D1539784

PORTFOLIO ASSESSMENT

Applications of Portfolio Analysis

Edited by

Michael E. Knight
Denise Gallaro

KEAN COLLEGE OF NEW JERSEY

UNIVERSITY
PRESS OF
AMERICA

Lanham • New York • London

Copyright © 1994 by
University Press of America® Inc.
4720 Boston Way
Lanham, Maryland 20706

3 Henrietta Street
London WC2E 8LU England

Library of Congress Cataloging-in-Publication Data

Portfolio assessment : application of portfolio analysis / edited by
Michael E. Knight, Denise Gallaro.
p.   cm.
1. Portfolios in education – United States.   2. College students –
United States – Rating of.   I. Knight, Michael E.   II. Gallaro,
Denise.   III. Title : Application of portfolio analysis.
LB1028.P67P66   1994   378.1'67—dc20   93–39233 CIP

ISBN 0–8191–9415–8 (cloth : alk. paper)

 The paper used in this publication meets the minimum requirements of
American National Standard for Information Sciences—Permanence
of Paper for Printed Library Materials, ANSI Z39.48–1984.

Contents

Contributing Authors

Polly Ashelman, Ed.D., Assistant Professor
Departmentof Early Childhood and Family Studies

Maureen Barron, M.A., Associate Professor
Department of Health Information Management

Virginia Fitzsimons, Ed.D., Professor
Department of Nursing

Denise Gallaro, M.A., Administrative Assistant
Office of Institutional Research

Martin Holloway, M.F.A., Associate Professor
Department of Communications and Theatre

Ted Hoyle, D.M.A., Professor
Department of Music

Michael Knight, Ph.D., Professor
Department of Early Childhood and Family Studies

Paula Kramer, Ph.D., Professor
Department of Occupational Therapy

Robin Landa, M.F.A., Professor
Department of Fine Arts

Rosalyn Lenhoff, Ed.D., Assistant Professor
Department of Early Childhood and Familty Studies

Holly Logue, M.T.A., Assistant Professor
Department of Communications and Theatre

Cathleen Londino, Ph.D., Professor
Department of Communications and Theatre

James Murphy, Ed.D., Professor
Department of Communications and Theatre

Dula F. Pacquiao, Ed.D., Assistant Professor
Department of Nursing

Janet Prince, Ed.D., Professor
Department of Instruction, Curriculum and Administration

Freda Remmers, Ed.D., Associate Professor
Department of Communications and Theatre

Susanna Rich, Ph.D., Associate Professor
Department of English

Natalie Sartori, M.A., Assistant Professor
Department of Health Information Management

Karen Stern, M.S., Associate Professor
Department of Occupation Therapy

Introduction

Michael Knight and Denise Gallaro

In education, the word "portfolio" traditionally refers to -- or brings to mind -- a collection of a student's writing samples. This definition may be appropriately applied in some academic areas, but not in others. There is a need for a broader definition of the concept of "portfolio" in areas such as art, theater, graphic arts, photography and the like. An expanded definition of portfolio including the collection of students' "work samples", such as student performance evaluations, simulations, interviews, role-playing, etc. Portfolio, as used in this context, will be the focus of this volume. For our purposes, we will use the broadest possible definition of portfolio, and encourage faculty to also use this perspective.

PURPOSE

The purpose of portfolio assessment is to enable faculty to assess the progress of individual students and the effects of programs across the broad spectrum of student development. That is, for students experiencing college, what portfolio information might we/should we gather in order to provide them with feedback that will improve their performance and positively influence their attitudes and perspectives toward themselves, toward others, and expand their career opportunities and life.

In a somewhat similar manner, faculties need to gather information, over time, related to the significant goals and objectives of their educational programs. Just as portfolio information is gathered about individuals to provide a basis for determining student growth and development, an assessment approach that gathers a variety of student work samples in a sequential manner can be used as a diagnostic tool to examine the educational program and make recommendations to enhance the quality of that program.

An initial step in portfolio development for either individuals or programs is to answer the questions listed below:

** How can appropriate samples of data be identified?
** Who will collect information for the portfolio?
** Who will maintain the information collected?
** Where will the information be stored?
** How will the rating system be developed? and
** Who will develop it?
** Who will validate it?
** How can we ensure the reliability of the rating system?
** Who will set the standards for acceptable program performance?
** How will this be done?
** Will the "evidence" produced be convincing?
** How will we validate the process?
** Is the evidence clear enough to act upon?
** If so, who will act?

An attempt to answer these questions -- and others, will clarify the process of portfolio assessment through all five stages of development as follows:

1. Development of goals and objectives - What should be incorporated in the process?

2. Instrument development

    A. How can we identify appropriate samples (products) of work?
    B. How can we develop and validate the rating system for individual work samples?

3. Data Collection - Who will collect and maintain the portfolio?

    A. Students?
    B. Faculty?
    C. Department Chair or Coordinator?
    D. Others?

4. Data Analysis

    A. How can we set standards or expectations of performance for individual students at the program level?
    B. How will you weigh the evidence?
    C. How will you validate the process?

5. Use of Data

    A. Will you act based on the evidence gathered?
    B. Will you act based on your analysis of the data?

According to Forrest (1990), a major purpose of engaging in program evaluation is to improve the program. A logical first step for any institution might be to begin to determine or define the program. Three common conceptions can be identified:

1. Coursework only -- institutions would seek information on only these courses and would use that information in structuring course requirements, designing courses, and modifying teaching styles.

2. Courses plus selected out-of-class activities -- evaluate the influence of out-of-class experiences on the achievement of other academic goals.

3. *All* elements of the college experience -- general education, elective coursework, coursework in the major field, extra-curricular activities are essential to achievement.

Why would students want to participate in such a process? Several reasons come to mind. The portfolio will effect their grade; it will enable students to better understand their own development (How am I doing?), and it is a product or a collection of products to present to potential employers or graduate schools.

Why would an academic program want to do this?   Faculty views of portfolio assessment include the idea that portfolio construction and assessment require constant "tinkering" by faculty and students to reflect current needs, pedagogies, and technical resources.   In adopting a portfolio assessment procedure for monitoring student progress and placing students in courses that reflect their needs, we empower not only faculty but students, as well, in a dynamic learning environment that requires and therefore develops constant critical thinking.

Specifically, a developmental writing course might respond that current timed placement tests for developmental writing students create tension and thereby poorer performance.   When the focus for placement is a timed test at the end of a semester, too many students may cut classes, which further exacerbates their problems.   Timed placement tests emphatically do not reflect the real nature of the writing process which requires work over time, consulting with others to develop a sense of purpose and audience, revising, letting it rest, and so on.

On the other hand, portfolio assessment of developmental writers -- which includes papers, revisions, and student self-assessment -- provides a holistic and realistic instrument for encouraging student output and diagnosing accurately skills to be further developed.   Students' self-esteem is much enhanced because -- instead of writing on a topic they wouldn't choose and about which they haven't had the time to think -- students create volumes of work which reflect their needs, passions, and individual styles -- volumes of which many of them can be proud. Most importantly, in developing portfolios over time, students learn the values of patience, responsibility, discipline, and commitment to their own development. In short, portfolios empower students.

A music department is considered an academic department, and in reality teaches a discipline that is not only academic but rather one that involves performance as well as academic knowledge.   It therefore, seems only reasonable to assess music students by means of a portfolio that includes examples of their knowledge of the academic areas of music.

In a music department, the main motivation for doing an extensive portfolio assessment is to discover and document how well students are learning the material that professors endeavor to teach them.   This feedback is invaluable because it indicates strengths and weaknesses in students and programs.   The

results can be quite surprising, but always helpful for building a stronger department.

Faculty are empowered by portfolio assessment, as well. The confer regularly with each other to shape and reshape the requirements of portfolio construction and assessment, thereby enhancing both pedagogy and morale. Developmental studies programs are habitually staffed mostly by graduate students and adjunct faculty. Providing an assessment instrument that requires networking is not only vitally important -- it's crucial to a successful program.

PIECES IN A PORTFOLIO

In a *work sample* a learner performs task(s) in a realistic setting which are observed and rated by evaluators. Work samples can be either simple or complex depending upon the expected learning outcome. They can allow programs to measure what individual learners can do and how this learning can be applied; flexibility, problem-solving and creativity; and levels of self-confidence in novel situations.

Two or more learners interacting in assigned roles exemplifies a *role-playing* scenario. Role-playing may combine interviews, discussions, group problem-solving, defending a position, information gathering, etc. Outcomes such as interpersonal skills, ability to communicate, think, etc., in novel situations, and empathetic understanding are measured.

Simulations or scenarios are processes wherein the learner simulates a role or situation in which he/she is faced with a typical set of problems or issues and must handle them in a specified amount of time. The use of simulations is appropriate for assessing complex skills such as problem-solving, decision-making, and setting priorities. This method measures outcomes such as understanding of the scope of a problem, setting priorities, making decisions, and taking action.

Constructing, designing, painting, or composing a *product* allows students to demonstrate learning in other than written form. Assessment of the quality of a product may be difficult, and expert judgment is required. The ability to perform a complete task (not a simulation) would be the outcome measured.

Oral Interviews involve direct questioning in order to elicit responses to assess learner outcomes through oral communication. Interviews may be one-to-one or may be comprised of a panel. They can also be structured (planned questions) or unstructured (conversational). The interview method of measuring outcomes may be used to assess complex behaviors more quickly than with writing techniques.   The outcomes assessed would include the ability to communicate effectively, the ability to organize thoughts and express them clearly and rationally, and learner anxiety or self-confidence. Interviews allow assessors the opportunity to exchange and verify information, influence or change behavior, and diagnose problems.

Other pieces that could be included in either a student's portfolio or a program portfolio include: charts, checklists, inventories, activity records, logs, diaries, behavior journals, questionnaires, standardized tests, etc. -- or any product that could serve as a measure of performance.

In order to provide specific examples of Portfolio Assessment at both the individual and program levels, the following chapters provide a variety of examples from programs that are commonly found on numerous campuses. We have selected representative programs from the following areas:

Health Information Management
Public Relations
Music
Developmental Writing
Early Childhood and Family Studies
Theatre
Visual Communications
Elementary Education
Nursing
Occupational Therapy

References

Forrest, A. (1990). Time will tell: Portfolio-assisted assessment of general education. (with support from the Exxon Education Foundation). Washington, DC: The AAHE Assessment Forum, American Association for Higher Education.

Planning a Portfolio: Medical Record Administration/
Health Information Management

Maureen Barron and Natalie Sartori

BACKGROUND:

The Kean College Assessment program includes departmental liaisons who are required to participate in Assessment Sharing Sessions each semester with other departments. It was through these Sharing Sessions that we learned how some departments include student portfolios as part of their assessment activities. When approached to contribute to this Anthology on Portfolio Assessment, we agreed to write about our plans for building portfolios into our program. Even though we are novices at this concept, we have come to believe that not only will the academic program be enhanced, but that faculty and students will benefit as well. We are in the early planning stages and are intrigued with the idea of our students having their own individual portfolio to demonstrate their professional competence at the time of a job interview.

At the time of this writing we are conducting a self study for Accreditation purposes. The portfolio concept will facilitate the process now and continue to be an ongoing assessment tool long after the survey team is gone.

MISSION OF THE MEDICAL RECORD ADMINISTRATION PROGRAM:

Through a curriculum based on the Professional Entry Level Competencies and Domains, as published by the American Health Information Management Association (AHIMA), the Medical Record Administration (MRA) faculty strive to impart values, skills and knowledge to the students to prepare them to meet the needs of the healthcare industry in the area of health information management.

Whether in hospitals, ambulatory care or alternate settings where health information is developed, maintained and applied, the MRA graduate will be able to manage health information systems consistent with the medical, administrative, ethical and legal requirements of the health care delivery system.

At the conclusion of the educational experience, the graduates will demonstrate high ethical standards regarding the personal and aggregate use of health information.

GOALS:

1. To prepare graduates to be competent in all the basic functions of management as specified in the Entry Level Competencies (Domains, Tasks and Subtasks).

2. To prepare graduates to ethically guide, control, influence and enforce policies related to the use of health information.

3. To prepare competent leaders in personnel administration.

4. To prepare graduates to develop, implement and maintain health information systems.

5. To prepare graduates to define, monitor, collect, retrieve and maintain healthcare documentation in accordance with standards of accreditation and regulatory agencies.

6. To prepare graduates to accurately collect, analyze, interpret and present data to support the health information needs of the health care organization both internally and externally.

7. To prepare the graduates to competently apply classification and indexing systems for the purpose of supporting research, health care services, planning and reimbursement.

8. To encourage the students and graduates to participate in, contribute to and assume leadership roles in the field of Health Information Management.

9. To foster attitudes that lead to a concern for continuing professional and personal education, growth and the pursuit of scholarly activities.

Objectives of the Medical Records Administration Program:

After completion of the program of study, the graduate will be able to:

1. Plan and Develop: Health information systems which meet standards of accrediting and regulatory agencies; training and development materials for instruction of health care personnel; departmental budgets; policies and procedures including those relating to medical-legal issues.

2. Design: Health information systems appropriate for various sizes and types of health care facilities; health record abstracting systems; departments in which health information services may be offered.

3. Direct: A total health information system appropriate to the facility; preparation of research indices; collection and analysis of patient care data; the management of human resources.

4. Participate in and Coordinate: Committee functions relating to medical records and patient information systems; medical staff activities in the evaluation of patient care and resource utilization; basic and applied research in the health care field; the services of the health information department with other departments in the facility.

5. Apply technical skills: Analyze and evaluate health records according to standards; compile and utilize various types of administrative and health statistics; code diagnoses and procedures; appropriately release health information; validate discharge data abstracts; maintain special registries.

How Will the Portfolio Fit into the Curriculum?

As we explored the concept of a portfolio and its value as an assessment tool it became apparent that many student projects are suitable and could easily be incorporated without alteration. Further analysis proved that it would be more difficult to limit the components of the portfolio rather that finding representative work samples. As a result it was decided that there were several advantages to slowly phasing in the assignments.

* First, we felt the probability for a successful portfolio assessment program would be increased. It is preferable to prudently select key assignments that reflected broad areas of student knowledge. This would improve the quality of the portfolio and prevent failure because of a new and overwhelming project.

* Second, as individual faculty members proposed an assignment as a potential portfolio item there would be incentive and opportunity to evaluate the quality of that assignment as a learning tool.

* Third, it would give us ample opportunity to rationally develop, review and/or modify the assignments that would become a part of the portfolio. The faculty feel that thorough communication regarding the portfolio components will be an important step in the success of this project. The opportunity for increased communication and discussion would in itself foster improvements in the assignments thus becoming an inaugural phase of assessment.

* Finally, a "slow" phase-in would allow a more detailed and exhaustive discussion and analysis of the assignments with the Advisory Board. The Advisory Board is composed of individuals who represent segments of the community that have interest in contributing to program development and support. See Table 1 for a listing of the "Communities of Interest." This added benefit was felt to be important because the Advisory Board will be a vital part of the process in two ways; a) Board members are an

important link to the "real world" for which we are preparing our students, and b) the Advisory Board would help measure the appropriateness, validity and reliability of each assignment.

In summary, the selection process will look at every course in the Medical Record Administration curriculum. Each professor will select one or two assignments from each class for review and evaluation as a potential component of the portfolio. Assignments will be appraised based on content and value as a valid and reliable assessment tool. To date the selection process has resulted in a preliminary list of three projects and papers that have been presented to the Advisory Board for comment and approval.

The preliminary list includes; a) student evaluations from two of the clinical affiliations, b) a student questionnaire, and c) scores from the comprehensive examination. Figure 1 contains a sample of the revised evaluation that is used for the first and last clinical affiliations to provide comparative data to monitor professional and technical growth.

Table 1. COMMUNITIES OF INTEREST

1. Hospitals
2. Prospective Students
3. Current Students
4. Past Students
5. New Jersey Health Information Management Association (NJHIMA)
6. Clinical Sites
7. Pharmaceutical Companies
8. Review/Consulting Agencies
9. Non-Acute Care Facilities
10. Other Schools
11. High Schools
12. New Jersey Hospital Association (NJHA)
13. Department of Health
14. Guest Lecturers
15. American Health Information Management Association (AHIMA)

Figure 1. Student Evaluation Form.

STUDENT NAME _____   DIRECTED PRACTICE I _____

FACILITY _____   MANAGEMENT AFFILIATION _____

MEDICAL RECORD ADMINISTRATION PROGRAM
KEAN COLLEGE OF NEW JERSEY

STUDENT EVALUATION

DIRECTIONS: Please indicate your professional assessment of
                the student by circling the appropriate letters.

    S.A. = Strongly Agree   A   = Agree   D   = Disagree
    S.D. = Strongly Disagree   N.O. = Not Observed or Not
Applicable

COMMENTS: Any additional information will assist in the
           development and assessment of the student. (S.A. and
           S.D. should be supported by comments when possible.)

1. Student adapted well to his/her   S.A.   A   D   S.D.   N.O.
    role in the department.

    Comments: _____

2. Student displayed appropriate   S.A.   A   D   S.D.   N.O.
    behavior in dealing with
    director/supervisor.

    Comments: _____

3. Student displayed appropriate   S.A.   A   D   S.D.   N.O.
    behavior in dealing with employees.

    Comments: _____

4. Student displayed self-   S.A.   A   D   S.D.   N.O.
    assurance in his/her abilities
    and knowledge.

    Comments: _____

5. Student demonstrated the   S.A.   A   D   S.D.   N.O.
    ability to follow through
    on activities as assigned.

    Comments: _____

6. Student displayed an   S.A.   A   D   S.D.   N.O.
    effective and efficient
    use of time.

    Comments:_____

7. Student willingly and con-   S.A.   A   D   S.D.   N.O.
    scientiously completed all
    tasks and activities assigned.

    Comments:_____

8. Student was able to discuss   S.A.   A   D   S.D.   N.O.
    assignments and departmental
    procedures objectively.

    Comments:_____

9. Student displayed good working S.A.   A   D   S.D.   N.O.
    habits in completing assignments.

    Comments:_____

10. Student assignments appeared   S.A.   A   D   S.D.   N.O.
    professional and neat.

    Comments:_____

11. Student was able to accept   S.A.   A   D   S.D.   N.O.
    constructive criticism.

    Comments:_____

12. Student demonstrated adequate   S.A.   A   D   S.D.   N.O.
    attentive and oral communication
    skills.

    Comments: _____

13. Student was a good listener and   S.A.   A   D   S.D.   N.O.
    at appropriate times.

    Comments:_____

14. Student worked quietly without   S.A.   A   D   S.D.   N.O.
    inappropriately disrupting work flow.

    Comments:_____

15. Student conveyed an even dis-   S.A.   A   D   S.D.   N.O.
    position.

    Comments:_____

16. Student was eager to assist in   S.A.   A   D   S.D.   N.O.
    departmental functions.

    Comments:_____

17. Student demonstrated initiative   S.A.   A   D   S.D.   N.O.
    and ability to solve problems
    independently.

    Comments:_____

18. Student showed autonomy in   S.A.   A   D   S.D.   N.O.
    learning activities when
    appropriate.

    Comments:_____

19. Student offered pertinent sug-   S.A.   A   D   S.D.   N.O.
    gestions to resolve problems.

    Comments:_____

20. Student asked relevant   S.A.   A   D   S.D.   N.O.
    questions regarding activities
    and tasks.

    Comments:_____

21. Student thoroughly completed   S.A.   A   D   S.D.   N.O.
    each task as expected before
    moving on to subsequent assignments.

    Comments:_____

22. Student desired to learn from   S.A.   A   D   S.D.   N.O.
    mistakes and accepted advice
    regularly.

    Comments:_____

23. Student was punctual for   S.A.   A   D   S.D.   N.O.
    meetings and did not exceed
    lunch and break times.

    Comments:_____

24. Student was able to establish a S.A.   A   D   S.D.   N.O.
    good rapport with departmental
    employees.

    Comments:_____

25. Student observed pertinent   S.A.   A   D   S.D.   N.O.
    rules and regulations.

    Comments:_____

26. Student demonstrated ability to S.A.   A   D   S.D.   N.O.
    apply past experiences and
    knowledge to present situation.

    Comments:_____

27. Student demonstrated a desire   S.A.   A   D   S.D.   N.O.
    to work at maximum potential.

    Comments:_____

28. Student demonstrated the   S.A.   A   D   S.D.   N.O.
    ability to conceptualize the
    effects of individual tasks in
    department and/or organization
    as a whole.

    Comments:_____

ADDITIONAL COMMENTS:

Would you hire this student?   **YES** _____   **NO** _____ .

If yes, in what capacity?

CLINICAL SUPERVISOR _____   **DATE** _____

STUDENT _____   **DATE** _____

Figure 2.   Comprehensive Examination Scoring Guide.

	Name		
CATEGORY	**NUMBER OF QUESTIONS**	**NUMBER CORRECT**	**PERCENT CORRECT**
Management	58	_____	_____
Legal Aspects	19	_____	_____
Personnel Admin.	25	_____	_____
Health Info. Systems	30	_____	_____
Health Records	26	_____	_____
Information Retrieval and Retention	20	_____	_____
Health Statistics	23	_____	_____
Quality Assurance	22	_____	_____
Classification Systems	12	_____	_____
Coding Problems	15	_____	_____
Total	**250**	_____	_____

How is it Used?

Our primary objective for incorporating the portfolio is to facilitate and improve the assessment activities of the department.   With total faculty participation in the systematic analysis of the portfolio, modification of the curriculum will be more organized and goal oriented.   This analysis will be accomplished through a succession of focused and broad reviews of portfolio components.   Results of this structured review will help meet our primary objective and also realize many supplemental benefits that are discussed later in this chapter.

The framework for portfolio is as follows:

1.   First, as mentioned previously the initial review would be conducted by individual faculty members. This will occur when a professor proposes an assignment for incorporation into the portfolio. As faculty consider an assignment it will be a catalyst to review the assignment for content and quality of learning objectives and competencies. After this initial examination faculty would formally propose the assignment for consideration at a departmental assessment meeting.

2.   At the departmental meeting the assignment would be scrutinized and discussed from several perspectives. First, is the assignment appropriate for the portfolio and if so can it be improved to better meet learning objectives. The assignment will also be discussed as to how it relates to other assignments and/or courses. Areas of duplication can be identified and assignments can be logically integrated to develop and build upon professional skills, theories and values. Another benefit is that faculty members will become more familiar with all course content as well as the interrelationship among various courses.

3.   More extensive and encompassing reviews would occur annually at departmental meetings. This meeting will have two focal points. Initially we will look at individual portfolios to assess a student's strengths, weaknesses and progress toward professional skills, values and competencies. Results of this meeting will be documented in a progress report to be reviewed with the student in a follow-up meeting. The portfolio will provide an objective medium for the student and faculty to conduct a self examination of strengths and weakness. Faculty and student discussion would yield constructive criticism and develop plans for improvement. In addition, the student will have the opportunity to make constructive comments regarding improvements for the assignment. The second focus would be holistic and comprehensive focusing on the collection of assignments and measuring the degree to which competencies for entry level health information managers are met.

4.   Finally we felt it was appropriate to include the Advisory Board at various levels of portfolio review. Through Advisory Board input, individual assignments could be discussed as to how they relate to the "real world." It also provides the Advisory Board with the opportunity to provide input and valuable information that lead to assignments that better prepare students to meet competencies.

What Does the Program and the Student Gain?

Data gathered through Assessment Activities continues to show "students lack confidence in their own achievements" (Kean College Assessment News, 12/1991).

They don't know what is expected in job market, so are not confident that their preparation is comparable or adequate relative to competition.

The MRA Program has much to gain by the implementation of a portfolio approach to student assessment. Some of the most obvious gains are:

1.   Outside participation in the development of criteria for professional practice standards.

2.   Development of indicators that can also be useful for faculty intervention as the student progresses through the program.

3.   The demonstration projects/portfolio components can be kept contemporary through collaboration with outside practitioners.

4.   Advisory Board members and the clinical site supervisors can assist in developing criteria for professional practice relevant and specific to the various types of healthcare facilities.

5.   The timing of a finished product (a portfolio component) may coincide with the student's job search and may therefore, influence the successful placement of graduates.

6.   Employment opportunities may be enhanced at the site of an affiliation for the students.

7.   Faculty and students both benefit from being able to monitor progress relative to program goals and objectives as driven by the Professional Competencies (Domains, Tasks and Subtasks).

8.   Portfolios provide an opportunity to keep communicating program goals to students so they can develop a point of reference for their own competency development.

9.   Since some of the components will result from clinical assignments, the student is provided a valuable opportunity for timely feedback from the Clinical Supervisor on the level of compliance with professional standards.

10.   Reinforcement and support for the student learning and therefore, enhanced self confidence.

11.   Students are provided opportunities to compare themselves with their peers.

What Does Our "Community of Interest Gain?

Because Advisory Board members often are representatives of the "Community of Interest" there is mutual benefit from participation in portfolio development. They influence the standards of quality against which the young professionals will be measured. It is through their participation that the standards developed can be practical, timely and appropriate. Potential employers will benefit by being able to differentiate between candidates' preparedness by reviewing work samples provided by the applicants. It may be likely that for a student to present a portfolio to a potential employer will be the exception rather than the rule and will give both a slight edge in the process of selection. The interviewer will be able to quickly assess strengths or weaknesses in the candidate by seeing projects or documents related to the student's professional coursework.

In summary, they:

1.   influence the development of outcome indicators relative to professional competency of new graduates

2.   are presented with a standard set of works from the Kean College of New Jersey (KCNJ) MRA graduates and can therefore, differentiate between applicants more readily

3.   can "mentor" newly graduated employees by having seen demonstrated strengths and weaknesses through the portfolio assessment.

Why Would a Portfolio be Credible as an Assessment Tool?

The professional world of Health Information Management would consider the portfolio credible for some of the following reasons:

1.   It is defined and developed through academic and professional practice collaboration and is based on professional Entry Level Competencies.

2.   Some of the component parts are developed during affiliations when the work would be evaluated by the Clinical Site Supervisor as well as the professor from the MRA Program.

3.   Given that the portfolio would meet generic needs of most facilities, it is likely that it would be transferrable knowledge and skills to a specific healthcare facility.

4.   It would contribute to the student's professional self-confidence by allowing them to bring their own "tools" to the job.

5.   Use of similar evaluations over time are valuable when validated by "experts" e.g. Advisory Board and faculty.

6.   It sets the student apart from other employees because they come with some demonstrable managerial, technical and academic accomplishments relative to their new profession.

FUTURE:

Where will we be with Portfolio Assessment two years from now? With the continued involvement of the whole faculty, interested students serving on the Advisory Board and an appropriate representation from our "Community of Interest" we will continue to work towards enhancing the student's self-confidence in their own professional abilities.

The Public Relations Portfolio

Freda L. Remmers and Cathleen Londino

Background:

Public Relations is one option within the B.A. in Communications offered by the Department of Communications and Theatre. The public relations portfolio assessment is one part of the total program assessment of the communications major. The complete assessment process is described in detail in <u>Outcomes Assessment at Kean College of New Jersey: Academic Programs' Procedures and Models</u> (Remmers and Londino, 1991). Program goals (see Table 1) were established in the beginning of the assessment process. The senior portfolio is the portfolio graduates present when interviewing for jobs, and it also represents a "final check" of how well students and faculty meet pertinent goals.

Table 1.   Communications Program Goals for Students and Faculty.

Goals for Students

Upon completion of the major, students will be able to demonstrate:

1. A basic understanding of mass media in the United States, including functions, economics, regulations, and constitutional issues
2. Critical thinking ability
3. Ability to analyze audiences and adapt messages to them
4. Persuasive ability — implementation of sound persuasion principles
5. Ability to support arguments
6. Flexibility in thinking
7. Argumentation skills
8. Ability to analyze issues
9. Competent writing skills
10. Interpersonal communication skills
11. Small group communication skills
12. Leadership skills in small groups
13. Ability to perform needed roles in small groups
14. Listening skills
15. Presentational communication skills
16. Ability to be a critical consumer of communication
17. Knowledge of ethics and professional standards
18. Ability to understand and communicate the meaning of written material
19. Knowledge of rhetorical and communication theory
20. Basic understanding of communication research
21. Knowledge of cross-cultural communication

<u>Goals for Faculty</u>

1. To guide students in attaining the above goals
2. To provide academic and career counseling for each student at least once each semester
3. To instill in students a commitment to lifelong learning
4. To instill in students a commitment to community service, both during college and in their future careers.

Portfolio Survey:

During the fall 1991 semester, a survey was completed of thirty public relations practitioners in New York and New Jersey (the most frequent job markets for our graduates) working in the following areas of public relations: corporate, agency, educational, nonprofit, government, and political. The respondents were alumni of the program now in management positions, managers who have hired our graduates, managers who accept our cooperative education interns, and managers who serve as guest lecturers in our public relations classes. The survey (Illustration 1) asked respondents to indicate what items should be included in the portfolio of an entry-level job applicant and to list the criteria on which respondents evaluate portfolios.

Illustration 1. Section I. Public Relations Portfolio Survey.

I. When you interview a job applicant for an entry-level public relations position in your organization, what items should be included in the applicant's portfolio? Please indicate the importance of each item in the list below by using the following scale:

      1 = must be represented
      2 = would be nice to see, but not crucial
      3 = not important

In the number column, please indicate how many of that item should be included.

Import	Item	No.
_____	News release	____
_____	Feature release	____
_____	Photo cutline	____
_____	Press advisory	____
_____	Pitch letter	____
_____	Article for in-house publication	____
_____	Clippings of published releases	____
_____	Speech	____
_____	Video script	____
_____	Slide show script	____
_____	Public service announcement	____
_____	Brochure copy	____
_____	Printed brochure	____
	Others? Please list	
____	_____	____
____	_____	____

Illustration 1. Section II. Criteria for Evaluation of Portfolio

---

II. Please list, in order of importance, the criteria you use to evaluate a portfolio. What specific qualities are you looking for in the applicant's writing? (Please list as many as you wish.)

1._____

2._____

3._____

4._____

5._____

6._____

7._____

8._____

9._____

10._____

Thank you for your assistance. Please return your completed survey in the enclosed self-addressed envelope.

The surveys were anonymous, but return envelopes were coded to indicate the area of public relations in which the respondent works. Follow-up telephone calls stressing the importance of the study were made one week after the surveys were mailed. Response rate of the surveys was 100 percent.

Section I of the survey, asking what items should be included in the portfolio, was analyzed, and a portfolio preparation guidesheet for students (Illustration 2) was prepared from the results. Section II of the survey, asking for evaluation criteria was analyzed, and a portfolio evaluation (Illustration 3) was prepared from the results. The twelve criteria represent the areas of highest agreement of respondents. In fact, most of the criteria appeared on 100 percent of the responses. The criteria also are consistent with the department's goals for students.

Illustration 2. Public Relations Portfolio Preparation

When you interview for a job in public relations you must present a portfolio for review. What you include in your portfolio will depend on the area of public relations in which you are interviewing. Please use the following as a guide to what your portfolio should include.

Corporate or Agency Public Relations

2 news releases
1 feature release
1 cutline
1 article for in-house publication
2-3 clippings of published press releases
1 press advisory
1 copy for brochure

  optional items
1 video script
1 speech
1 printed brochure

Nonprofit or Educational Public Relations

2 news releases
2 feature releases
2 cutlines
1 article for in-house publication
2-3 clippings of published press releases
1 press advisory
1 slide show script
2 public service announcements
1 copy for brochure

  optional items
1 speech
1 printed brochure

Government or Political Public Relations

3 news releases
1 feature release
2 cutlines
2-3 clippings of published press releases
2 press advisories
1 pitch letter
1 slide show script
2 public service announcements
1 copy for brochure

  optional item
1 printed brochure

Illustration 3. Public Relations Portfolio Evaluation.

Student _____   Date _____

Evaluator _____

On a scale of 1 to 5, how successfully does the work in this portfolio meet the following criteria:

	Highest				Lowest
1. Shows creativity	1	2	3	4	5
2. Shows a variety of work	1	2	3	4	5
3. Shows knowledge of correct style	1	2	3	4	5
4. Is well-organized	1	2	3	4	5
5. Shows clarity of writing	1	2	3	4	5
6. Shows conciseness of writing	1	2	3	4	5
7. Is adapted to audience	1	2	3	4	5
8. Is persuasive	1	2	3	4	5
9. Uses correct grammar	1	2	3	4	5
10. Uses correct spelling	1	2	3	4	5
11. Has good lead paragraphs	1	2	3	4	5
12. Looks neat and professional	1	2	3	4	5

Portfolio Preparation:

During their senior year, most students concentrating in public relations enroll in the elective capstone course, Public Relations Writing, where they compile a portfolio of written work. In fact, the items on the portfolio preparation guidesheet are the requirements for the course. Each student takes on a client, usually nonprofit, and completes all writing assignments for that client. The portfolio is composed of selected pieces of writing.

Seniors not enrolled in the course prepare, with individual assistance from faculty, a portfolio of writing based on internship work, class assignments from communications courses, practicum projects, work at the campus newspaper, and work at the campus radio station.

Beginning in the spring 1992 semester, students were given a portfolio preparation guidesheet and an evaluation form when they first express an interest in the public relations component of the department. Each student in the department must meet with his or her faculty advisor at least once each semester. During these advisement sessions, public relations students bring in any work they have done that might be suitable for their portfolios, and their work is discussed with their advisor. This way, students who are unable to take the capstone course will have a head start in preparing their portfolios. Also, on occasion, a student applying for an internship is asked to submit a portfolio. The work in the portfolio done to date should prove ample for this purpose. Students are responsible for keeping their own portfolios, but if they request it, copies of their written work are kept in their advisement files.

Portfolio Evaluation:

Students in the Public Relations Writing course have one day at the end of the semester designated as portfolio review day. Final portfolios are due on that day. Seniors not in the course are also invited to bring their portfolios for review. During that class period, each student evaluates three other students' portfolios, using the portfolio evaluation form. Forms are handed in after each evaluation, so the next evaluation is not biased by a previous evaluation. Following this class, the professor of the course evaluates each portfolio, using the same instrument. Then two public relations practitioners who volunteer for the task evaluate the portfolios, using the same instrument. Evaluation results are returned to the students, and the course professor works with students individually to correct any deficiencies found through the evaluations. This portfolio evaluation process and the instrument are being tested at this writing. Following the evaluation, the results will be analyzed for inter-rater reliability.

Implementation of Survey Results:

The portfolio preparation guidesheet has already proved useful for graduating seniors. It gives them concrete information, so there is no longer any guesswork involved in preparing their portfolios. They also have the advantage of knowing exactly how their portfolios will be evaluated by job interviewers. Students just beginning in the major now have specific goals set for them in terms of work they must accomplish during their years in the major. They also know what work they need to save for possible portfolio use.

The survey results also led to some changes in the teaching of the Public Relations Writing course. For example, students still learn the basics of the routine writing that public relations practitioners do, but since 93 percent of respondents indicated creativity was the number one criterion they look for, much greater emphasis in the course is placed on creative writing. The importance of the lead paragraph was being taught, but since 83 percent of respondents listed good leads in their top three criteria, more class time is now devoted to writing leads. In fact, a reporter for a large daily newspaper now visits the class and evaluates students' lead paragraphs on both news and feature releases.

Some course requirements have also been changed. Previously, students were required to write a thirty-minute speech. Since the survey showed a speech was important only in government and political public relations (fields in which very few of our graduates look for jobs) the assignment was changed to a ten-minute speech, and students are encouraged to write a speech for use by a government or political figure. Previously, students had the option of writing either a video script or a slide show script. The survey showed a slide show script is important in all areas except corporate and agency. There a video script is optional (listed by less than 33 percent of respondents). Also, students are exposed to video scriptwriting in two other major courses. So the assignment was changed to require a slide show script.

Relationship to Program Goals:

The portfolio process does help students meet the first nine goals for students set by the department. By definition, public relations writing is persuasive writing, where arguments must be supported and issues and audiences analyzed. Writing is done for various media and must be appropriate for each medium. Critical thinking and flexibility in thinking are shown in the approaches and angles chosen for each piece of writing.

The process also helps faculty meet the first, second, and fourth goals set for them by the department. The portfolio process requires constant, individual attention and guidance for each student. Also, since much of the portfolio writing is done for very grateful nonprofit organizations, students see first-hand the value and importance of community service.

In short, the portfolio process is important not only in preparing students for their future careers, but in meeting the program's goals for both students and faculty.

Portfolio Assessment in the Music Department

Ted Hoyle

The most important information needed in order to understand portfolio assessment in the Music Department at Kean College is the goals of the program. The following are those goals:

GOALS OF THE MUSIC MAJOR AT KEAN COLLEGE:

A. Performance on major instrument

1. Intonation (where applicable)
2. Rhythmic accuracy
3. Beauty of tone
4. Musicality
5. Difficulty of repertoire

B. Theoretical knowledge of Western music

1. Key signatures
2. Major and minor scales
3. Intervals
4. Figured bass
5. Four part harmonization of melody
6. Analysis of form and harmony
7. Knowledge of basic orchestration (required of music ed. majors, others urged to take this course also)

C. Sight-singing and dictation abilities

1. Tonal melodies (using sol-fa syllables)
2. Complex rhythms
3. Melodic dictation
4. Harmonic dictation

D. Historical knowledge of Western music

1. Stylistic trends of each major historical period
2. Major composers of each major historical period
3. Principal genre of each major historical period
4. Ability to discuss aspects of music history in well written prose

E. Music Education methods (music ed., majors only)

1. Vocal K-12
2. Instrumental K-12

F. Functional piano ability (required of music ed. majors only)

1. Ability to play patriotic songs
2. Ability to play from a simple score
3. Elementary knowledge of keyboard harmony

The Music Department of Kean College considers the comprehensive file which we maintain on every music major a portfolio of that student's progress while in our department. It contains each semester's grades, all programs of musical performances in which that student has participated at Kean College, all jury, forum, and recital performances. All performances have evaluation forms as well as the corresponding videotapes of that student's performances while enrolled in the Music Department. Thus, for every student who enters the Music Department as a music major, we start a portfolio which, by the time the student graduates, contains a considerable body, both videotaped and written, of various samples of their work during the time that they were a student in our department.

Every student who applies for admission to the department is given an audition on their major instrument which is videotaped and independently adjudicated by at least two faculty members using a specific performance-evaluation form. (See the sample form included at the end of the chapter.) The music faculty developed this form as a result of assessment activities. A student whose performance abilities do not measure up to our criteria-referenced standards is advised not to become a music major, but instead to become a music minor or simply to take music courses on an elective basis. In addition, we require all incoming students to take placement exams in music theory, music history, sight-singing, and piano proficiency. These exams are adjudicated using the same basic system that we use for every aspect of music department assessment which is blind readings by at least two faculty members and rating the exam on a scale of 1 to 5, with 5 being the highest. Comments are encouraged. Thus we have the first entry in that student's portfolio which indicates the incoming musical abilities of that particular student. Note that this material is gathered before they have attended their first class at Kean College. This knowledge about each student is of great benefit for advisement purposes, and of course for carefully following the progress of that student.

The fact that our department is small allows us to video and adjudicate all individual performances of our students throughout their enrollment in the department. These performances include jury exams at the end of each semester, required informal recitals, which we call Music Department Forums -- all students are required to attend these forums and they are also required to perform on a forum program at least once every year; and the culminating performance for each student, the senior recital, a formal solo recital. A member of the Music Department Assessment Committee coordinates all videotaping with the cooperation of the private teacher of the student performing. Each student has his/her own videotape (or tapes) and two performance-evaluation forms for each taped performance which are kept in a file or portfolio in the office of the Music Department, and to which the student and private teacher have easy access. We also maintain a file of videotaped performances of all Music Department ensemble performances. This documents how our students perform in ensembles; groups that are taped include the Women's Chorus, the Chamber Music Ensembles, the Kean College Concert Band, the Brass Ensemble, the Guitar Ensemble, the Percussion Ensemble, and the Jazz Band. We also videotape our annual Madrigal Dinner.

It is easy to see that with our extensive use of video we are able to completely document a student's performance growth during their study in the Music Department. Apart from the various ensemble performances in which a student participates there are a minimum of thirteen solo videotapes of each student during the four years that they are in the department. The Assessment Committee picks at random one performance from each academic year and of course the senior recital as the performance component for that student's portfolio. Each of these performances has two independent performance-evaluation forms completed by two faculty members, and it should be noted that over four years the students have many different faculty members adjudicating them, so there is an overall consensus of opinion.

As noted above, the performance-evaluation form was developed over several years at the onset of the assessment process in the Music Department. All faculty members participated in the development of this form and while we may change this form again in the future, it seems at present to fulfill our needs adequately. No mere form will ever be able to totally indicate something as abstract as a musical performance, just as the written word cannot capture the true essence of a painting, however with a videotape of that performance the written evaluation can become much more accurate and meaningful.

The Music Theory component of the portfolio contains the incoming theory placement exam as well as a comprehensive examination that every music major is required to take after they have completed a specific sequence of required theory courses. This exam is given in most cases at the end of the junior year. The Music Department feels that it most important to wait a semester or two after a student has completed the required sequence before assessing the student. Knowledge and skills that have really been retained are more easily discerned than if we gave the exam directly after the courses were taken. The exam is about two hours long, and covers all of the goals and materials indicated in the Music Department goals for music theory, sight-singing, and dictation. These goals are also in agreement with the goals of our accrediting agency, the National Association of Schools of Music (NASM). The exam is given blind readings by two members of the music theory faculty. Each rates the exam on a scale of 1 to 5, with 5 being the highest. Comments are encouraged. Students are advised of the outcome and may see the exam if they wish. Weaknesses are discussed and appropriate advisement is given to correct these weaknesses during the next year. Consistent and widespread weakness in a particular area indicates that more emphasis is needed in the classroom and the instructors are expected to address this shortcoming.

The Music History component of the portfolio contains the initial placement exam as well as a comprehensive assessment exam in Music History. This exam is structured in much the same way that the theory exam is structured. Several semesters after the student has completed a sequence of required courses in music history, a two hour exam covering all areas of the Music Department goals for music history knowledge is administered. The exam is given blind readings by two members of the music history faculty and rated on the same scale as the theory exam. Comments are encouraged. Appropriate advisement is given the student, and they are encouraged to remedy any serious deficiencies in the following semesters. Again, as with music theory, classroom emphasis is adjusted to reflect needs indicated by these exams. **It should be noted that as**

the assessment process at Kean College is NOT a gate, we cannot force a student to take remedial action, but merely to advise them to do so.

Music Education majors have two additional components in their portfolio in addition to all of the above. This reflects the Music Departments goals for the Music Education major which reflect NASM recommendations, New Jersey state requirements, NCATE requirements, and NTE requirements. The first component is a comprehensive one hour written exam on vocal and instrumental education methods (K-12). This exam also covers material on basic orchestration. The exam is given blind readings by two music education faculty members and rated on a scale of 1 to 5 as in all written exams in Music Department Assessment. Comments are encouraged and advisement is given each student by the coordinator of Music Education. The second component is a functional piano jury. Each student plays a 15 to 20 minute functional piano jury for two music education faculty members including the coordinator of Music Education. This jury covers the goals for functional keyboard skills set by the Music Department. A Functional Piano Evaluation Form is filled out independently by the two faculty members. (This form was developed especially by the Music Education faculty at Kean College for the assessment process. It is somewhat different from the regular Performance Evaluation Form as functional piano requires different skills.) Appropriate advice is given each student concerning each of these two music education components.

The faculty of the Music Department of Kean College feel that we have developed a reliable and valid assessment method for assessing the programs and outcomes of most aspects of our music majors' education. To be sure, some of it is subjective as we are dealing with a most abstract and subjective discipline, however we, as a faculty always agree with each other as various members of the faculty undertake the task of rating and assessing different aspects of each students' education. We also have frequent conferences about particular students in the monthly faculty meetings. Is this method specific? It is 100% reliable? Is it 100% valid? Of course not, and it can never be, but for the present we feel that we have a very workable assessment method. In five years there will no doubt be changes as the need arises, but certainly using the portfolio method for assessment will remain as it is the most reliable documentation for students' progress.

Figure 1. New Student Application.

Please Complete and Return

Kean College of New Jersey
Music Department

Supplementary Application for Admission to Undergraduate Study

Please Complete and Return To:
Music Department
Kean College of New Jersey
Union, N.J.   07083

SS# _____   Date of Entrance _____

Semester & Year

1.   Name _____   Age _____
        Last Name   First Name   Middle or Maiden

       Address _____   _____
            Street & Number   City   State   Zip   Tel. No.

2.   Secondary School & Graduation Date _____

3.   Specific Major: (Please Check)

            B.A. _____   Music Education _____   Music Liberal Arts

4.   Major Instrument or Voice _____

            Number of Years performing experience _____

            Number of Years Private Study _____   With Whom? _____

5. Number of Years formal and/or informal study in: Music Theory _____

6.   Check One: I plan to appear at the scheduled audition time _____

                I prefer to attend a later audition _____

Admission to the Music Department will be held until you have attended one of the scheduled auditions.

Your acceptance to the college is subject to approval by the OFFICE OF ADMISSIONS.
If you have any questions, please call the Music Department 527-2107/08

Figure 2. Performance Evaluation Form.

Date _____

AUDITIONS   JURY   FORUM   RECITAL

Name _____ Age _____ Instrument _____
      Last Name   First

Status: Freshman   Sophomore   Junior   Senior   Transfer   Certification

Number of Years of Study _____   Teacher (with whom) _____

1. Not acceptable 2. Needs Improvement 3. Satisfactory 4. Very Good 5. Excellent

Scales						
_____						
intonation	1	2	3	4	5	NA
tone quality	1	2	3	4	5	
accuracy	1	2	3	4	5	

Composition						
_____						
intonation	1	2	3	4	5	NA
rhythm	1	2	3	4	5	
accuracy	1	2	3	4	5	
tone quality	1	2	3	4	5	
musicality/interpretation	1	2	3	4	5	

Composition						
_____						
intonation	1	2	3	4	5	NA
rhythm	1	2	3	4	5	
accuracy	1	2	3	4	5	
tone quality	1	2	3	4	5	
musicality/interpretation	1	2	3	4	5	

Composition						
_____						
intonation	1	2	3	4	5	NA
rhythm	1	2	3	4	5	
accuracy	1	2	3	4	5	
tone quality	1	2	3	4	5	
musicality/interpretation	1	2	3	4	5	

Profile (general)						
sight reading (if applicable)	1	2	3	4	5	NA
stage presence	1	2	3	4	5	
estimated potential (audition)	1	2	3	4	5	
achieving at expected level (juries)	1	2	3	4	5	
additional comment (if necessary)						

Faculty Member _____

Figure 3. Music History Audition Exam.

I.   Listening: Identification of three famous works (composer and name of work)

      1. _____
      2. _____
      3. _____

II.   Define the following:
      1.   Sonata

      2.   Recitative

      3.   Opera

      4.   Concerto

      5.   Suite

III. Match the composer with the period

      1. _____ Debussy   A. _____ Medieval
      2. _____ Schoenberg   B. _____ Classical
      3. _____ Palestrina   C. _____ Modern
      4. _____ Mozart   D. _____ Renaissance
      5. _____ Bach   E. _____ Romantic
      6. _____ Beethoven   F. _____ Baroque
      7. _____ Machaut   G. _____ Impressionist

IV.   Name the composer who is particularly associated with the following:

      1. Impressionism   _____
      2. Twelve Tone Technique _____
      3. Fugue   _____
      4. Leitmofiv   _____
      5. Rubato   _____

V.   Answer the following:

      1. What instruments make up a string quartet?

      2. What is the name of the oldest body of Western monophonic music?

      3. Define SYMPHONY. Give the usual sequence of movement in this genre.

Figure 4. Functional Keyboard Proficiency Audition.

Student _____ Date _____

Prepared Composition _____ Rating _____

Sight Reading _____ " _____

Transposition (music) _____ " _____

        (orig/key:) _____ (intvl, direction
                    of transposition) " _____

Scales _____ " _____

Arpeggios _____ " _____

Recommendation:	Beginner	(Mus 1511	CIP	I
(circle appropriate	Intermediate	12		II
Rom. Num)	Advanced	13		III
		14		IV

                    Auditioning Jury: _____

                                    _____

                                      _____

                                      _____

Test Me, Test Me Not:
The Portfolio Alternative for Developmental Writers[1]

Susanna Rich

A large room is shared by two groups assessing the work of developmental writers. The outcome of this end-of-semester evaluation session will be to pass individual writers into the regular college composition course or to recommend that they remain in the developmental writing program for an additional semester.

The members of the first group are distributed at the far corners of two large rectangular tables strewn with stacks of blue examination books, neat clumps of rubber bands, and hills of paper clips. Hunched over the bluebooks, the evaluators do not talk with each other--though a moan or a giggle will bubble out from time to time. They read their assigned essays, record and cover their numerical scores, and pass stacks of bluebooks to the group leader. This person monitors the passing of the bluebooks so that no evaluators read works written by their own students. A graduate assistant then records the numbers on print-out sheets. This orderly scene soon succumbs to entropy: Heads droop onto the pedestals of arms, backs lean against walls, legs shift and wiggle--yawns, sighs, knuckles cracking. The session coordinator casts an insistent yet apologetic glance at two readers who are chatting over a student essay. "Take a break," she says. "No that's OK--we want to get these over with," they say, glancing over at the members of the other group.

The members of the other group are talking animatedly in pairs and fours around two other rectangular tables stacked high with manila folders, blue sheets, and student papers. They call or walk to members of other groups, laugh, puzzle, read papers aloud, compare them to other papers. "Sometimes it helps to put students in pairs," one instructor is saying, "Especially E.S.L. students--large group workshops may be embarrassing at first." "Jocelyn is a go-getter," another says, "She went from fragments to complex sentences in one semester. I'm sure she'll go to tutorials on her own for this spelling." The coordinator calls for the next stage of the process to begin. It takes a few

[1] My thanks especially to Priscilla Donenfeld and Sue Woulfin, and to Maryellen O'Shea, John Wargacki, Anthony Agresta, Janet Giardina, and Sylvia Mulling for their enthusiasm, insights and dedication to the developmental writing program at Kean College, and the portfolio project, in particular.

minutes before the members of this assessment team are willing to turn their attention away from their folders to the coordinator, who, meanwhile, is drawn into one of the conversations over a given set of papers. Another one of the small group members teases her out of it, "Really now. We just can't get your attention."

This essay describes and compares the first, traditional assessment system of scoring timed placement tests, as portrayed by the first group, and the second, a portfolio assessment system being piloted in the Developmental Writing Program at Kean College of New Jersey.

Traditional Placement Tests

Description:

Incoming students are required to take state-mandated writing tests which serve as placement indicators for college writing courses. The New Jersey College Basic Skills Placement Test is divided into a 20-minute essay written in response to a single prompt and a 40-minute 40-item multiple-choice "sentence sense" portion. Some colleges use this instrument for exit criteria for passing developmental writers, as well. Because of the stress on objectivity, the administration and evaluation of these placement tests have been strictly monitored. The essay prompt is a closely guarded document. Tests are distributed and collected under conditions replicating the administration of S.A.T. tests. Students know, as they are writing, that they will never see either their essays again or more than a score by way of evaluation.

Scoring is even more carefully conducted. The state distributes a group of "range finders"--student essays which represent a range of abilities. Scorers read these unmarked essays and assign to each a score of a low of 1 to a high of 6. Zero is assigned to some essays which don't respond to the prompt and do not merit even a "1" for the writing. These tests are scored "holistically," that is, to reflect not merely grammar, punctuation, and spelling, but more importantly for such qualities as depth of thought, logic of argument, and use of evidence. The numerical score, then, is meant to reflect the overall ability of the writer. Another approach to the assignment of scores is to assign "3" to essays that indicate a student belongs in a developmental writing course, and "4" to essays that merit placement in the regular college curriculum. Once the scorers have assigned scores to these range-finder essays, they compare their results and discuss criteria they used, so as to achieve a balance in perspective among the group members. Range-finding is the only time during the assessment process when scorers freely discuss essays.

Student essays are then distributed to readers who have not had direct experience with the student writers--that is, no instructor will be scoring the work of her or his students. Also, instructors should not know the identity of the instructors of the students. Each student essay gets two readings--the scores for which will not be available between readers. If a numerical score differs by more than one point, the essay goes to a third arbitrating reader. This scoring system requires a complex of tasks including shuffling, tracking, clipping, distributing, reshuffling, recording, and interpreting numbers. The sentence sense portion of the test has to be scantroned and numbers have to be further interpreted.

Advantages:

The hoped-for benefit of this instrument was to provide

1) an objective instrument for placing student writers,
2) data for evaluating student progress,
3) data for evaluating writing programs.

Disadvantages:

Students and instructors object to traditional timed placement tests for many reasons:

1) Environment. Timed tests are administered in highly artificial, often unfamiliar settings--hectic, crowded with many nervous student writers. This does not replicate the natural settings for the writing process as writers, scholars, and other professionals know it. Most writers write in environments they have either designed to support their writing or which they have learned to ignore.

2) Time. The time limitation can actually induce writer's block. As one student put it, "What can you do in twenty minutes?" Another complains, "The faster I write, the more my writing ability deteriorates." Most good writing is done over a span of time which allows for incubation of ideas, collection of supporting

materials, false starts, consultation with others, revision, typing, proofreading. Nonetheless, studies have shown that allowing more time for writing under test conditions--up to 75 minutes--actually resulted in poorer scores for some students.

3) Topics. Engagement is essential to good writing. All writers--especially apprentice writers--need a wide range of topics from which to choose. In fact, one of the main skills of writers is to choose and focus topics that energize and inspire them. Many of the topics provided in timed tests are foreign to the writers, who justly resent having to expound on issues that do not concern and often befuddle them.

4) Self-esteem. As writer Logan Pearsall Smith put it, "The great art of writing is the art of making people real to themselves with words." Timed placement tests--coming at the beginning of college careers--can be especially devastating to the self-esteem of new writers. The act of writing is an act of assertion. To fail a student on the basis of timed tests is tantamount to saying, "What you have to say is not good enough--you aren't really there." Furthermore, students are disenfranchised from their own work because they never see either their test essays or qualitative explanations of their scores.

Some students are poor test-takers but competent writers. Misplaced students can become very discouraged and therefore resistant to writing if they too judge their abilities according to artificially created writing conditions. To be judged by a timed test after a semester of engagement in generative writing activities is a betrayal.

5) Pedagogy. An assessment instrument should measure what it claims to measure. Timed placement tests do not measure either how students learn or what abilities they have developed. During a productive semester in a writing course, students will focus and refocus essays; collect ideas; organize and reorganize their work; consult with peers, tutors, instructors, family and friends on their papers; read models for inspiration; experiment with different approaches; draft and redraft; transform some halting starts into engaged prose and abandon others; revise, edit, and proofread. Through this process, student writers will learn to identify with and be sensitive to audience and purpose in their writing. In short, they will have adopted the strategies of practicing writers. Timed tests do not measure the student's ability to act as a writer in these many ways. Nor do timed placement tests reflect the major bulk of writing that students will be required to do either in college or in their professions. Even short essay exams allow time for students to collect and consider the ideas they

will be asked to write upon. Term papers should never be written in one sitting, but drafted and revised over at least half a semester.

An assessment instrument should ideally generate data which will lead to improved pedagogy. Timed placement tests have led to the teaching of such stilted writing strategies as the five-paragraph essay. Instructors "teach to the test" by drilling students in points of grammar, punctuation, and spelling. These drills, supported by workbooks, are not merely ineffective--in many instances, they are counterproductive. As one student put it, "I can do it all right in the workbook. It's just that I can't do it in my own writing." To write effectively, students need to learn how to think, not merely to write one word answers to prefabricated sentences that they would never write themselves. Students need to become aware of their writing habits so that they can adjust their own work. They also need the freedom to make mistakes without fear of premature judgment. Timed placement tests produce two most unfortunate by-products: first, high absentee rates among students during their developmental writing course, because students feel they can just show up for the test; second, bright, innovative instructors with otherwise genuine commitment to developmental writers too often leave developmental writing courses. These instructors cannot tolerate the tests, the scoring procedures, or the pedagogy that the tests seem to require. The result is that the students who need to practice writing the most do not show up. The instructors that could most effectively model and encourage students through the writing process may not be there to teach them for long.

6) Reliability. A good test-taker can pass the timed placement test but be incapable of writing more than a mechanically error-free paragraph. So some students are prematurely passed into the regular college writing course. They fail. They do not have recourse to the support system provided by a developmental writing program (including tutors and freedom to experiment). A poor test-taker may nonetheless be a skillful writer, given the opportunity to work under conditions natural to the writing process. If these otherwise competent writers are held back, they can lose momentum and motivation to improve their writing.

No matter how carefully readers are trained in scoring, the process is unreliable. Scoring and interpreting the work of 400 students--comprising 800+ readings to be completed under highly-controlled conditions--is a daunting, tedious, and thankless job. As instructor Sue Woulfin reports:

No matter how we try to be fair, I know that I'll either become easier or harder on the students as time drags by. I'm only human. I also worry about the fate of these students even though they are anonymous to me. Failing anyone tested under stressful conditions seems wrong.

7) <u>Program Assessment</u>. An assessment instrument should not only improve pedagogy but energize a whole program of writing instruction. Timed placement tests are a bane to students, instructors, and coordinators alike. They do not test what they are meant to test. Nor do they improve instruction. They do,however, produce neat columns of numbers which can easily be manipulated to assess the success of writing programs. Since the tests do not reliably pass deserving student writers, the short-as well as long-term results of instruction in a writing program cannot be fairly assessed through the scores generated by the tests.

Portfolio Assessment

Description:

In portfolio assessment, portfolios of student work are the major instruments used for assessing and placing students. Students are accountable for focusing, collecting, organizing, researching (if necessary), drafting, revising, editing, and proofreading work in their own portfolios. In the process of developing their portfolios, students collaborate with each other in peer groups and develop language skills in the way language skills are actually acquired: through consistent practice in a community of writers. The portfolio may include in-class essays, as well.

A portfolio assessment system requires that faculty be trained throughout the semester in evaluating their teaching and the effect it has on student writing. They meet at the beginning of the semester to organize, in the middle to adjust, and at the end to assess portfolios. For objectivity, instructors work in teams so that they can 1) decide on the **contents** of the portfolio, 2) formulate and reformulate **criteria** for success in writing, 3) adjust and readjust their **pedagogy** in response to students' progress and responses, and 4) evaluate the assessment **procedures.**

Table 1 shows the "Portfolio Contents Checklist" developed during the pilot year of portfolio assessment in the Developmental Writing Program at Kean College. Most instructors required students to type all their drafts for many reasons: typed drafts are easier to revise; studies have shown that composing at keyboards encourages fluency; typed drafts are easier to photocopy and distribute for group review; typed drafts are easier to read; a polished presentation is a satisfying product for the writer.

The types of papers to be included in the portfolio are broadly defined to allow instructors and students to develop and focus engaging topics for writing. A major work of at least 5-7 typed pages challenges students to write in depth. At least two drafts are required for each paper. To encourage self-reflection, ownership, and awareness, students are required to write detailed letters assessing their own work. The checklist serves also as an itinerary of due dates that students and instructors negotiate together.

Table 2 shows the "Evaluation Criteria" list that both students and instructors use to assess writing. The three categories of criteria are "Process Evaluation," "Usage," and "Punctuation." The evaluation criteria are keyed to The Flexible Writer: A Basic Guide by Susanna Rich, published by Allyn and Bacon, 1992. The text was developed to reflect the experiences of instructors and students in the Developmental Writing Program, not only at Kean College, but many other institutions, including the University of North Carolina, New York University, Montclair State College (New Jersey), and Sussex County Community College (New Jersey).

Seven phases of the writing process--undertaken in varying order by writers with different styles and needs--are identified in the text: identifying purpose and audience, focusing, collecting, organizing, drafting, consulting, and revising. (See Table 3.) Even unskilled writers will be more proficient at one phase of the writing process than others; writer's block is defined as getting stuck in any one phase. During the semester, instructors help students identify those phases of the writing process which they need to further develop. Students then turn to particular chapters devoted to the phases they need to learn in more depth.

Table 1. Portfolio Contents Checklist

In this folder, submit the following pieces of writing. All final drafts must be typed. <u>Number</u> and <u>clip</u> drafts of each paper <u>under</u> the final version (with the first draft on the bottom of each group). Do not staple any papers. Papers from categories 1-3 must all include at least one revision each. How you construct your folder will be a reflection of your ability to work as a college writer.

1. _____ A personal/expressive piece which is primarily the result of your experience (at least 2-3 typed pages)

2. Do a or b (or both)

a. _____ A persuasive piece whose main purpose is to agree or disagree with some statement on a public concern (at least 2-3 typed pages)

b. _____ A piece of writing that is in response to some written document: academic, business, professional,historical, etc. (at least 2-3 typed pages)

3. _____ A major work which is longer and more completely revised than the others. This may be a series of papers on one subject or a longer paper. The focus of some paper written for 1 or 2 may serve as a basis for this paper. (at least 5-7 typed pages)

4. _____ Letter from the beginning of the course in which you relate your experience of writing and what specific skills you want to develop during the course. Use the criteria for evaluation listed in this folder. (This letter may be revised.)

5. _____ Letter from mid-semester in which you review your work in the present course and project what you want to accomplish, specifically, during the rest of the semester. Use the criteria for evaluation listed in this folder and cite specific examples from your papers. (This letter may be revised.)

6. _____ Letter of self-evaluation at the end of the course in which you specifically state what you have learned so far and what aspects of process, usage, or punctuation you need to work on. Use the criteria for evaluation listed in this folder and cite specific examples from your papers. (This letter may be revised.)

7. _____ Pre- and post- in-class writing samples (to be enclosed by your instructor)

Table 2: Evaluation Criteria

Evaluators: Please check areas for further development.

Process	1st	2nd	Punctuation	1st	2nd
Sense of Purpose	___	___	Apostrophe	___	___
Audience Awareness	___	___	Comma	___	___
Focusing (Choices, examples)	___	___	Semicolon	___	___
			Colon	___	___
Collecting (Depth, range)	___	___	Period	___	___
Organizing (Structure, transitions)	___	___	Question Mark	___	___
			Quotation Marks	___	___
Consulting	___	___	Hyphen	___	___
Revising	___	___	Dash	___	___
			Parentheses	___	___

Other_____

Usage

Fragments	___ ___
Run-ons	___ ___
Comma splices	___ ___
Verb agreement	___ ___
Verb tense shifts	___ ___
Pronoun agreement	___ ___
Pronoun shifts	___ ___
Spelling	___ ___
Vocabulary	___ ___
Other (diction, etc.)	___

Questions of usage and punctuation are questions of meaning. The handbook chapters of The Flexible Writer provide students with strategies for identifying and revising their usage and punctuation to most effectively satisfy the purpose of a given piece of writing. Instead of doing workbook exercises, students are invited to develop sensitivity and range with usage and punctuation by writing, consulting with others, and revising. Faculty in the developmental writing program meet mid-semester to discuss changes and refinements of both the Portfolio Contents Checklist and the Evaluation Criteria. This focus provides instructors with a context in which to discuss a wide range of theoretical, pedagogical, psychological, and practical issues. For example, instructors will discuss whether the purpose of a developmental writing program is to prepare students for academic discourse, or to help them develop a sense of community in a multicultural context. Instructors swap strategies for helping students develop a sense of audience through working in pairs or small groups.

Instructors commiserate over problems ranging from managing the paper load to managing resistant students. They also consider such detailed questions as whether the subtleties of the semicolon are daunting, or inspiring and interesting to developmental writers.

Table 3. The Writing Process.

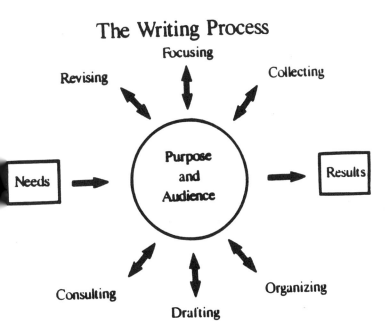

The Writing Process

Focusing

Revising

Collecting

Needs

Purpose and Audience

Results

Consulting

Drafting

Organizing

The culminating meeting of the semester is the final portfolio assessment meeting. Instructors prepare for this session by conducting a portfolio construction session with their students a week prior to the meeting (allowing time for strays, late-comers, last-minute revisions and proofreading). During the pilot of the portfolio assessment program at Kean College, students were also asked to write an in-class essay in response to their choice of two topics offered them. Approximately 75 minutes was allotted for the completion of these essays and dictionaries and thesauruses were available. This in-class essay was collected for two purposes--as additional data for evaluating the program, and as one additional piece of writing for assessing each student.

Instructors read through the portfolios of their own students and assign them to three categories: sure pass, sure fail, and not sure. In assigning portfolios one of these three categories, they consider whether the portfolio indicates that the student is ready for the regular college composition course. The portfolio assessment meeting starts with range-finding. Each instructor takes representative samples from the three categories and stacks the six portfolios in random order. Then instructors pair up with other instructors (usually a more experienced instructor will join a newcomer) and swap their stacks of six portfolios. They read the six and assign them categories, as well. Then they discuss their assessments of them.

In plenary session, instructors articulate the criteria they used to assess their own and others' student portfolios. Criteria are recorded on a board, both to be available during the session and to invite additions. During the pilot program, these were some of the criteria recorded for

Failing	Passing
--incomplete folders	--clean and complete presentation
--lack of development	--steady improvement
--inability to recognize own problems (as reflected in letters to instructor)	--a sense of responsibility towards own work
--cryptic	--fluent, longer papers
--dull, cliché	--energy, originality
--no sense of audience	--engaging, sense of audience

Some additional questions instructors asked themselves and each other were: Could this student survive in composition? Would another semester yield only diminishing returns given the apparent psychology of this student? Would I be willing to have this student in a regular college composition course?

Following the range-finding portion of the meeting, instructors form groups with one or two other instructors. Again, experienced and new instructors will be encouraged to find each other--experienced instructors offer precedents, new instructors a fresh perspective. These groups will then assess unsure folders only--assigning pass or not pass. Together they will weigh factors and invariably add additional criteria to the list developed during range-finding. As follow-up to the semester, students are asked to sign a release form indicating their wishes regarding the disposition of their portfolios (see Table 4). This is a necessary step to honor students' right to privacy.

Advantages:

Portfolio assessment offers advantages in the very areas in which timed placement tests present disadvantages:

1) Environment. The portfolio is comprised of papers and letters written in the kinds of environments in which students will be writing during their college careers.

2) Time. Students write as other writers do--over a span of time which allows for the individual writer to move among the phases of the writing process as it is most productive for her or him.

Table 4. Release Form

Kean College of New Jersey
Developmental Writing

PORTFOLIO ASSESSMENT

Release Form

I, _____ , agree to have my portfolio of work from the
         (Print full name)
_____ semester of _____ passed on to my next writing instructor in order that
she or he may be better able to help me develop my writing skills.

Signed _____   Date _____

****

I, _____ , do not agree to have my portfolio of work from
         (Print full name)
the _____ semester of _____ passed on to my next writing instructor. I will
make appropriate arrangements through my present instructor to retrieve my portfolio (minus the
in-class essays). If I do not retrieve my portfolio within six months after my signing this form,
I understand that my portfolio may be discarded.

Signed _____   Date _____

---

3) Topics. Students learn to focus on and develop topics that most fully engaged
them, just as most successful writers do. They also have the time to formulate
and develop engaging points of view in response to topics which may not have
originally inspired them.

4) Self-esteem. At the end of the semester, each student has a consolidated
product to show for her or his efforts. This, in itself, can be very motivating and
satisfying. "I never knew I could write this much," students often say. "It didn't
seem possible that I could revise my first stuff into something that's good."

Allowed to develop their own interests and strengths and to learn strategies for transforming problems into opportunities, students develop the confidence of their own voices. Because they are not judged on work written under conditions that put them at a disadvantage, students feel they have a fair chance to accomplish their academic goals.

In addition, the portfolio assessment conducted during the pilot at Kean College actively involved students in shaping and assessing their own work. Through this, they developed one of the most important characteristics of a writer--the ability to judge and be responsible for one's own work. The results of the portfolio assessment procedure rarely come as a surprise to either the instructors or the students because the assessment proceeds throughout the semester.

5) Pedagogy. Portfolio assessment radically improves student attendance, not only because students couldn't rely on the test but because of the opportunities provided in the process of preparing portfolios.

Since the construction of the portfolio is the focus of the semester, portfolio assessment measures--as an effective instrument must--what it claims to measure. In addition, the instrument generates data which helps instructors to better address the needs of their writing students.

Because portfolio assessment requires constant consultation among students, students and instructors, and instructors with each other, pedagogy changes and improves to reflect the real needs, abilities, and resources of students and instructors, alike. Developmental writing programs are predominantly staffed by adjunct faculty and/or graduate assistants. Portfolio assessment fosters a community which allows participants to share ideas: people are energized through these interactions and their self-esteem is much enhanced. Whereas timed placement tests tax instructors so much that they leave the developmental writing program, the pilot at Kean College sufficiently interested instructors who were not teaching developmental writing to join the meetings.

6) Reliability. The evaluation processes of both the traditional and the portfolio teams are called "holistic." But the scoring of timed tests is holistic only in a limited sense--each score represents both qualitative and mechanical features of the writing. Students never see their own tests or benefit from the evaluation. None of their other traits, crucial to writing--such as responsibility, perseverance,

commitment, capacity for improvement--can be considered. Instructors not only do not but must not either assess or comment on their own students' work. Both students and instructors are disenfranchised from their work. Presently, data is being collected for assessing longitudinally whether portfolio assessment is more reliable for placement than timed placement tests. However, one thing is reliable--the portfolio system itself has markedly increased the engagement of students in their own writing. Since writing improves through writing, this instrument is more reliable as a pedagogical support.

Disadvantages:

7) Constant Refinement. Timed placement tests form a neat system which, once instituted, can be mechanically reproduced semester after semester. Portfolio assessment requires constant refinement every step of the way by everyone--from students, through instructors, coordinators and administrators, and back. But this "disadvantage" is happily accepted by all because it energizes everyone--teaching and writing are treated as arts, not assembly lines.

8) Program Assessment. Timed placement tests disenfranchise administrators of developmental writing programs, especially since funding has depended on tabulatable results. On the other hand, portfolio assessment does not, and is not likely to produce neat columns of scores which can easily be manipulated to assess the success of writing programs. However, longitudinally, we may find that students who participate in a writing program which relies on portfolio assessment are more likely to succeed as writers in the regular college curriculum.

Further Challenges:

The next set of challenges for portfolio assessment in developmental writing is to develop a system by which students can continue, throughout their college careers, to use the portfolio as a tool for learning. These are some questions that must be answered:

1)   Who keeps the portfolio?
2)   How would portfolios be stored for easy access?
3)   What are students' rights concerning privacy?
4)   Who would consult the portfolios after the student passed into the regular college curriculum?

5)   How could portfolios be used to bridge courses within the English or Writing department?

6)   How could portfolios be used to bridge courses across the curriculum?

7)   What are the parameters for refining the system?

8)   What resources are available for funding portfolio assessment?

9)   How are these systems to be assessed? How is data to be collected?

10)   Which, if any of these initiatives should be given priority?

Summary

A cartoon in the April, 1992 NCTE publication, The Chronicle, compares assessment and tests through two images. In one, entitled "testing," a man under gloomy skies--lines of worry scoring his forehead, eyes half-shut--yanks at the petals of a daisy while mumbling "yes, no, yes, no, maybe, all of the above." A woman in the background is doing the same. A rabbit in the corner comments "Seems pretty hit-or-miss to me." In the adjacent cartoon, entitled "assessment," two broadly-smiling characters under a sunny sky scoop armsful of daisies and seem to be enjoying the aroma. The caption that bridges both images is "Springtime: a time to stop and smell the flowers."

Writers flourish in environments natural to the writing process. Test them not.

Early Childhood Education

Polly Ashelman and Rosalyn Lenhoff

Everyone who teaches deliberates about how to maximize learning outcomes and encounters the recurring question "how do I do a better job?" In an effort to address these issues, members of the Department of Early Childhood and Family Studies designed a system of portfolio assessment which has become an integral part of the evaluation process for undergraduate and graduate students and the instruction program. Portfolios represent the intersection of assessment and instruction, and they provide a framework for viewing evaluation as a complex and multidimensional dynamic that emphasizes development of metacognitive strategies, empowerment and responsive program practice (Figure 1).

Figure 1. Conceptual Model. The intersection of assessment and instruction.

CONCEPTUAL MODEL

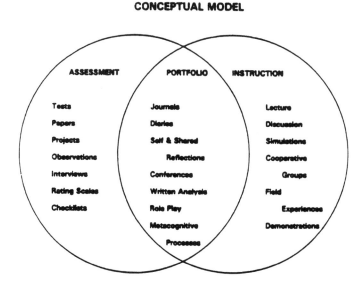

The model of portfolio assessment, used by the department, is based on the principles of constructivism (Kohlberg & DeVries, 1987; Kamii, 1988) and the research of Paulson and Paulson (1990). It includes a personalized approach to professional growth that is consistent with the faculty's beliefs about how children and adults construct knowledge and the strong connection between assessment and instruction. Also, it is in keeping with the growing use of portfolio assessment in early childhood practice, and provides our students with direct experience of portfolio development and analysis.

Portfolios provide a format for collaborative and systematic collection of data for reflection and analysis, development of professional growth plans, and verification of progress toward individual and program performance standards. This form of assessment includes both formative and summative information, addresses how individuals reason and engage in problem solving and creates a forum for facilitation of communication among colleagues that includes reciprocal feedback processes; thus, forging a partnership between faculty and students that promotes shared responsibility for learning and stimulating faculty interaction for purposes of program evaluation and revision.

Maintaining portfolios for graduate and undergraduate students serves three primary departmental goals. First, assessment for college students is congruent with the department's position on appropriate assessment strategies for young children. Second, instruction and assessment are based on a constructivist approach, which validates the importance of each student's role in self and shared reflection, goal setting and commitment to taking personal responsibility for professional growth. Third, assessment involves the faculty in a similar process of self-reflection and individual change, as well as a collegial process of modification of the overall program.

To help in development of a comprehensive system of constructing and evaluating portfolios, the department has adapted the Cognitive Model for Assessing Portfolios, developed by Paulson and Paulson (1990), which incorporates three dimensions: Activities, Historical and Stakeholder (Figure 2).

Figure 2. The cognitive model for assessing portfolios.

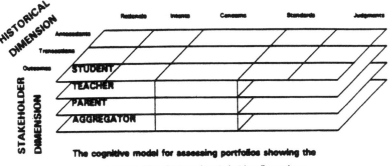

The cognitive model for assessing portfolios showing the
activity, historical, and stakeholder dimensions.

The Stakeholder dimension involves the relationship of mutual investment shared between each student and faculty advisor. Throughout their course of study, students work with the advisor to choose the samples for their portfolio which they feel best reflect their growth and professional development. Student choice supports the concept of active involvement in assessment, as an essential and vital part of the student's construction of knowledge. In addition, as the student and advisor work together to select and analyze information, each invests time and energy that deepens the commitment of both to continued professional growth.

The Historical dimension illustrates a tri-cycle temporal perspective which includes antecedents or a baseline record of performance, transactions, which document changes evidenced in portfolio samples over time, and summative information that can be used to verify outcomes. Products collected represent each of these three stages in each student's development.

The Activities dimension illustrates philosophy, describes what is actually found in the portfolio and what is minimally acceptable. Rationale is Why we assess. Intents describes What to assess. Content refers to Which specific samples of work. Standards relates to How good the level of performance is, and Judgment relates to If we reached our goal.

The content of the portfolio primarily involves the work of the students, as well as observational analysis of their performance in the classroom. Writing, Philosophy, Simulations, and Field Practice are the focused content.

The first activity to be examined is writing. Both students and faculty confer to clarify the process by which writing is to be judged. Samples of writing are collected at three specified intervals from a variety of contexts, are examined over time and are reviewed using criteria adapted from the Alverno College model as the primary source. This set of indicators includes organization, complexity, analysis, conventions, and context (Table 1). Sharing specific feedback and student analysis of models of effective writing are illustrative of strategies that are used to help students who need to improve their writing skills.

Table 1. Skills Assessment: Writing Assessment

```
1 = less exp.        3 = exp.
2 = mod. exp.        4 = excpt. exp.
```

	1	2	3	4

1. Reaching audience through ESTABLISH-
ING OF CONTEXT (sources of thinking,
documentation.)   ____ ____ ____ ____

2. Reaching audience through VERBAL
EXPRESSION (word choice, style,
tone, i.e. friendly, scholarly)   ____ ____ ____ ____

3. Reaching audience through APPRO-
PRIATE CONVENTIONS (usage, spelling,
punctuation, capitalization, sentence
structure, format)   ____ ____ ____ ____

4. Reaching audience through STRUCTURE
(sense of introduction/development/
conclusion; focusing by main point
made; paragraph).   ____ ____ ____ ____

5. Reaching audience through SUPPORT/
DEVELOPMENT (organization of ideas,
support the organization, idea
generation).   ____ ____ ____ ____

6. Reaching audience through APPRO-
PRIATE CONTENT (analytic approach,
problem-solving process).   ____ ____ ____ ____

General assessment of strengths and weaknesses (write in
paragraph form):

On the undergraduate level, specified writing samples include a research paper developed in four stages during the sophomore level, a lesson plan based on a case study developed during the junior year, and a narrative professional report to a child study team developed during the senior year. Students are also encouraged to submit additional examples of their work which they feel reflect their professional growth.

On the graduate level, there are three stages in the process of collection and assessment of writing. The first takes place during two specified courses, that are prerequisites for admission to the advanced level. In these courses a review of the literature and a research design are developed. The second occurs during completion of three additional required and/or approved elective courses. Within this stage, students choose samples for inclusion in their portfolio, which include a mini-research project, a comprehensive review of the literature, position papers, and essay tests. This stage culminates with a written comprehensive examination. The third includes the development of an Advanced Seminar research project to be written for a professional audience. This project is developed in cooperation with a committee of department members, who examine areas such as content, format, and style.

The second activity encompasses elements of professional development. Information collected includes development of a professional philosophy and growth plan. Each student's professional growth plan is reflected upon, utilizing structured teacher judgments based on a model developed from guidelines for professional development of the National Association for the Education of Young Children.

On the undergraduate level, sophomores complete a pre and post course self-assessment of motive and expectations called "Myself as Teacher." Juniors develop a paper on their philosophy of early childhood education; working from the abstract prior to their concrete field experience. Seniors complete a similar paper; this time basing their philosophy on their actual field placement connecting this concrete experience to theory.

Graduate students develop a professional growth plan which, in the first stage, includes goals for change during their course of study. This plan is formulated during the introductory course and is reviewed periodically. Each student develops a written professional philosophy, that connects theory and practice, during the next stage. The final stage is completed during the Advanced Seminar project. Each project must be shared with a professional audience through presentation of a workshop, implementation of a grant, preparation of a manuscript for a recognized publication, or innovative leadership contributions to a professional organization.

The third activity is simulated practice. On the undergraduate level, this consists of planning a unit or project in both the junior and senior years. These plans are implemented in classroom simulations. In addition, simulated practice dilemmas are a part of the seminars connected with field practice.

On the graduate level, students engage in various simulated activities that require them to reflect and act on the application of theory and current research in classroom or administrative settings. Examples of these are dilemmas or vignettes for discussion or role playing, curriculum design projects, and generation of plans for an innovative approach to teaching or administration.

The fourth activity is field practice. On the undergraduate level, students engage in field practice of increasing length and intensity in the sophomore, junior and senior years. In the sophomore year each student receives a checklist of performance behaviors developed by the department (Table 2). This is utilized in both the junior and senior field practice through a cycle of ongoing observation and feedback, video self-assessment, and mutual analysis.

Table 2.   Checklist of Performance Behaviors.

Student _____   Date _____

Cooperating Teacher _____   Jr. Field _____

College Supervisor _____   Sr. Field _____

Scale: (1) strong; (2) above average; (3) average;
        (4) below average; (5) (NA) not applicable

THE STUDENT TEACHER

(1)   1   2   3   4   NA   arranges the environment purposefully for
                            young children.

(2)   1   2   3   4   NA   searches out and provides various materials
                            using library and other resources

(3)   1   2   3   4   NA   presents the materials in ways that
                            stimulate interest, enthusiasm and curiosity

(4)   1   2   3   4   NA   organizes that materials in areas accessible
                            for children

(5) 1 2 3 4 NA   encourgaes children to bring their own ideas
                         to the use of materials

(6) 1 2 3 4 NA   uses a variety of multi-sensory, multi-media
                         materials and equipment, including computers

QUESTIONING SKILLS

(7) 1 2 3 4 NA   asks higher level questions: e.g. "What
                         if ...?, What do you think...?

(8) 1 2 3 4 NA   waits after asking questions in order to
                         encourage more participation

(9) 1 2 3 4 NA   adapts and re-asks questions based on
                         children's responses

(10) 1 2 3 4 NA   demonstrates respect for children and their
                         contributions

(11) 1 2 3 4 NA   accepts "wrong" answers and uses strategies
                         to discover child's reasoning

COMMUNICATION SKILLS

(12) 1 2 3 4 NA   develops the activity/lesson in such a way
                         as to promote the children's interest in
                         participating

(13) 1 2 3 4 NA   is clear in expressing ideas and concepts,
                         giving directions, and setting goals

(14) 1 2 3 4 NA   uses language appropriate for young
                         children; volume, grammar and vocabulary

(15) 1 2 3 4 NA   plans activities/lessons based on children's
                         abilities and experiences, going from the
                         known to the unknown

(16) 1 2 3 4 NA   responds sensitively to individual and
                         cultural differences

(17) 1 2 3 4 NA   develops the activity to extend
                         understandings and relates it to the child's
                         world

(18) 1 2 3 4 NA   recaps and integrates the activity/lesson so
                         children see the connections

(19) 1 2 3 4 NA   writes clearly and competently

(20) 1 2 3 4 NA   uses non-verbal communication, e.g. body
                         language, facial expression

CLASSROOM MANAGEMENT SKILLS

(21)   1   2   3   4   NA   provides sufficient time and space to explore ideas or materails for children in large and small groups

(22)   1   2   3   4   NA   provides children with sufficient feedback and positive reinforcement of their progress within the activity/lesson

(23)   1   2   3   4   NA   communicates clear expectations for behavior and achievement both before and during activities/lesson

(24)   1   2   3   4   NA   explores ways to provide assistance to children who exhibit learning problems

(25)   1   2   3   4   NA   plans activities/lessons to that children are not forced to wait too long until each has a turn

(26)   1   2   3   4   NA   assists children in making smooth transitions between activities

PROFESSIONALISM

(27)   1   2   3   4   NA   demonstrates a good relationship with colleagues

(28)   1   2   3   4   NA   acts as a professional, e.g. on time, prepared,...

(29)   1   2   3   4   NA   seeks, reflects and responds to suggestions

COMMENTS:

SUGNATURE_____

On the graduate level, most students are employed in early childhood settings and use those sites for required action research and curriculum projects. Since these students are not enrolled in a program that grants certification, the college does not supply support for supervision of field practice. Therefore, it has been necessary to devise an alternative system of review. A pilot under development is a three stage field practice assessment process that includes shared video analysis of the graduate student as a practitioner, on-site faculty and/or peer observation, and a documented statement about performance from the student's supervisor. Those students who are not employed complete these requirements in settings recommended by the department.

To implement the portfolio analysis process, the department established the following steps. All students are introduced to the portfolio process through an entry course that is identified at both the undergraduate and graduate level. At this time, faculty and students' responsibilities are specified and criteria for selection of samples are established. An advisor is assigned who will meet periodically with the student to review the contents of the portfolio.

Collecting and maintaining all samples that represent the activities dimension indicators is a cooperative process between the student and advisor. The advisor is responsible for maintaining each portfolio at a primary location in the department with access available to both students and faculty. Also, students are encouraged to maintain a copy of each selected work. At the conclusion of the course of studies on both the undergraduate and graduate level, all students have an exit interview with their advisor for the purposes of examining their own growth and reflecting on the context for learning provided by the department.

To pilot the full process of analysis with an advisor over the full course of studies, a random sample of 10% of the undergraduate students and 20% of the graduate students were selected. The larger percentage of graduate students was because of the smaller number of students involved. Therefore, each faculty member is the advisor for five undergraduate and two graduate students. Students meet with their advisor at least once a year for reflection, analysis and goal setting.

As a reliability check, another faculty member is invited by the student to be part of the Portfolio Review committee. This committee meets mid-point in each student's professional development; immediately following Junior Student Teaching for the undergraduate program and after successful completion of the comprehensive examination for the graduate program. Prior to the end of the program, the committee gathers again to determine whether the goals of the department and the student have been satisfied.

Having all faculty members involved in portfolio advisement has enabled heightened awareness of programmatic concerns and issues. Aggregation of the data serves to evaluate how well the program is meeting its goals. This process supports faculty reflection on whether existing instructional strategies point to consensus or compromise resulting in departmental changes or modifications.

Other problems and issues have been identified, as portfolio assessment has been phased into departmental practice. Addressing the standards and judgments in this model of assessment poses several dilemmas. The first is how to incorporate the highly personal and possibly divergent perspectives of both the student and the faculty advisor. The process of engaging students in self-assessment and reflection for the purposes of making judgments about their own work is highly individual and personal. It also requires high order thinking of critical awareness and nondefensiveness of one's evaluative strategies (Wasserman, 1991).

Whereas a traditional model of assessment focuses on standardizing knowledge of specific facts and skilss, portfolios focus on the processes the student goes through and the emerging ability to use strategies of metacognition. The outcome is "determined by human judgement ... and respects the human capacity for judgement" (Poulson and Poulson, 1990, p. 13).

Another dilemma is that the substantial variation in content found in individual portfolios will inevitably find diversity in analysis. The vary nature of the portfolio variance mitigates against traditional measures of reliability and validity. The more situations vary, the more traditional measures of reliability and validity will drop. The more authentic the personal variation, the less valid are traditional measures.

The last dilemma concerns appropriate utilization of data that have been collected. Ohlhausen and Ford (1990) describe four levels of utilization. At the Awareness level portfolios are seen as an assessment opportunity. At the Collection level, the portfolio is primarily a scrapbook without reflection. The Discovery level finds some reflection, but not goal direction. At the Actualization level students use the portfolio process to direct their own growth in order to change.

Achievement of the actualization level relates to the application of strategies of critical thinking and problem solving in professional life. This is the goal of the Department of Early Childhood and Family Studies portfolio assessment process.

References

DeVries, R. & Kohlberg, L. (1990). Constructivist early education: Overview and comparison with other programs. Washington, DC: NAEYC.

Kamii, C. (1989). Young children continue to invent arithmetic: Implications of Piaget's theory. NY: Teachers College Press.

Ohlhausen, M. & Ford, M. (1990). Portfolio assessment in teacher education: A tale of two cities. Miami, FL: Paper presented at the annual meeting of the National Reading Conference. (ERIC Document Reproduction Service No. ED 329917)

Poulson, L. & Poulson, P. (1990). How do portfolios measure up? A cognitive model for assessing portfolios. Union, WA: Paper presented at the Annual meeting of the Northwest Evaluation Association. (ERIC Document Reproduction Service No. ED 334251

Wasserman, S. (1991). What evaluation for? Childhood Education, 68, 2, 93-96.

Portfolio Assessment of the Theatre Program

Holly Logue and James Murphy

Introduction:

The assessment of the Theatre Program at Kean College began in the Spring of 1987. This coincided with the formation of a new Communications and Theatre department which was to occur in the Fall of 1987. (The program had been housed within the English Department for more than ten years as a Speech-Theatre-Media option.)

The Theatre assessment process has been slow and exploratory. It has led to the discovery of many questions and departmental strengths and weaknesses. The Kean Theatre Program is small, but growing, and attracts students with a variety of goals. At the time at which the assessment began our majors numbered 20 - 25. Our faculty has remained constant over the last five years at five full-time positions and one half-time position. The great advantage to this has been the ability to involve all of our faculty in the assessment of each individual major.

The areas to which we have devoted most of our attention include admission requirements, advisement, course sequencing, curriculum revision, individual progress review, recruitment and entrance and exit testing.

Development of a Portfolio Assessment Process

After researching comparative college theatre programs, we determined that a portfolio evaluation of each of our majors would be our primary assessment instrument. We have also been working on developing a written examination to test for cognitive skills information.

Briefly, our current portfolio evaluation consists of an audition and interview for those students who pursue the acting program, and a portfolio review and interview for those choosing technical theatre, design, directing or stage management. The audition or portfolio review and interview is video taped in one of the college's television studios to provide a record of the student's progress from the time they enter the program to the time they graduate. They are assessed in this manner once a year. A detailed description of this process will follow.

How Do We Assess the Portfolio Performance?

Each student prepares either a monologue of their choice from any work of theatrical literature or a portfolio presentation of their technical or directorial accomplishments. This audition/presentation is videotaped by the Kean College Instructional Resource Center Television Studio to assure a reasonably good quality.

During the portfolio presentation, faculty evaluators rate the students on a 1 - 5 scale based on successful demonstration of performance skills. In addition, consideration is given to year of study, courses completed, and practical experience.

Following the portfolio presentation, the student undergoes a five minute interview with the theatre faculty present. The interview questions, developed by the theatre faculty, include both general questions about their strengths and weaknesses, and specific questions about their participation in the program and their long-range career objectives. Questions and evaluation forms are included in Appendix A.

The video tapes are then kept by the faculty advisors and each student is asked to see his/her advisor to review and assess the tape. During this debriefing, the student and the faculty member evaluate the presentation in its entirety. Not only are performance skills addressed, but interview skills as well. Evaluation forms are reviewed, the answers to the interview questions are discussed, the choice of clothing worn, poise, choice of audition material and so on. At the end of four years, the student takes the videotape with them as a record of their growth.

In monitoring the progress of our students, we are learning where the program is strong and where we need to improve.

Who Is Assessed?

All theatre majors are assessed. Theatre minors are encouraged to participate but are not required to do so. When the secondary education collateral is in place, all theatre education majors will also participate.

When Does the Assessment Take Place?

New majors are assessed in the semester they enter, usually the fall semester. Transfers and current majors are assessed every spring semester.

What is Being Assessed?

The theatre faculty sees the theatre program as a microcosm of the world. A theatre student should not only develop performance or technical skills, but life skills. A theatrical performance requires teamwork, learning to put others first, a sense of community and loyalty, governance, accepting and fulfilling responsibilities, discipline, balance and creative and critical thought.

At first we are looking for a student's understanding of themselves as actors, designers, directors, etc. Their choice of material often reflects a knowledge of who the student thinks he/she is and how he/she expects to be perceived by others in terms of physical, vocal, and personality type.

Students are also directed to be able to realistically assess their strengths and weaknesses, maximizing the strengths, developing the areas of weakness. Although some students have natural instincts and are somewhat self-aware, for many, this is a difficult goal to achieve.

Both in the classroom and in their area of performance, an attempt is made to chart a course for each individual student which enables them to analyze their strengths and weaknesses. For actors, these include such skills as character analysis, observation, imitation, vocal variety, projection, articulation, physical coordination, pantomime, imagination, exaggeration, concentration, believability and the ability to know who they are as actors. Technicians are assessed by observing samples of their drafting, plots, elevations, renderings and so on. Directors and stage managers often display a production book. Throughout the student's four years with us, their skills are sharpened and honed as much as possible.

Finally, the portfolio assessment evaluates the student's confidence, poise, verbal expression, physical appearance and mastery of the subject (See Illustrations 1 and 2).

Illustration 1. Assessment Audition Form.

Name _____

Year of Study _____   Primary Interest _____

Intended Graduation _____   Today's Date _____

Theatre courses completed thus far:

Intro to Theatre	_____	Scenic Painting	_____
Acting I	_____	Summer Theatre	_____
Tech. Theatre	_____	British Theatre	_____
Theatre Lab (#sem)	_____	Dialects	_____
Directing	_____	Children's Theatre	_____
Acting II	_____	Kean Players	_____
Acting III	_____	Other related courses:	
Theatre History	_____	_____	
Acting/Profession	_____	_____	
Acting for T.V.	_____	_____	
Lighting Design	_____	_____	
Scenic Design	_____	_____	
Costuming	_____	_____	

General Education Courses:

Composition	_____	Emergence	_____
I.C.T.	_____	Landmarks	_____
I & R	_____	Science & Tech.	_____

Audition/Portfolio Evaluation

Monologue choice:	1 2 3 4 5	Portfolio:	1 2 3 4 5
Vocal Expression:	1 2 3 4 5	Organization:	1 2 3 4 5
Physical Expression:	1 2 3 4 5	Presentation:	1 2 3 4 5
Characterization:	1 2 3 4 5	Material choice:	1 2 3 4 5

Interview Comments

Confidence:

Poise:

Appearance:

Verbal Expression:

Mastery of Subject:

Illustration 2.   Sample Assessment Interview Questions.

Note: The questions are designed to reveal the students' personal knowledge as well as their familiarity with and understanding of concepts and objectives of classwork, production work, and production performance. We do not expect prepared answers from the students. Rather, we encourage truthful, open, and spontaneous responses.

First Round
1. Now that you are committed to this program, in what ways do you see yourself contributing to the success of the program and/or the theatre season?

> Possible follow-ups to No. 1 to determine the student's realization of responsibilities to the theatre series, the department, the school, the community.

> 1a. Do you see yourself participating on the theatre series council?
> 1b. Do you see yourself seeking a crewhead position?
> 1c. Do you see yourself seeking a position as an assistant to a director, designer, etc.?

2. What do you consider your strengths?

3. What weaknesses would you like to continue to strengthen?

4. Where do you see yourself ten years from now?

-

Second Round
1. How has your coursework helped you in the preparation and performance of today's audition/interview?

2. Now that you've been here for _____ years, in what areas do you feel most confident?

3. Based on what you've accomplished thus far, what are your goals for next year?

4. Last year your ten year goal was _____
    Has that changed? What steps have you taken towards achieving that goal?

Final Round - For graduating seniors
1. What were your most valuable experiences during your tenure at Kean?

2. Are there program changes you would recommend based on your experiences?

3. What is your immediate goal and how have you made plans to achieve it?

Impact of Portfolio Review

As a direct result of implementing the process of portfolio assessment, as delineated above, we have attempted to constantly review that process, the instruments used and all procedures employed. We have revised the rating/evaluation sheet several times based upon review of its use and effectiveness in achieving our goals.

We learned early on that we wanted close to ideal conditions for our tapings of each student. Initially we taped in any available classroom/theatre which resulted in very poor quality. By the second year we made arrangements with the campus Instructional Resource Center to use the college television studio for all of our assessment tapings. The result has been a much more effective final product through which the student can clearly examine his/her strengths and weaknesses.

We have clarified and established interview questions asked of each student at the conclusion of the prepared presentation. These questions are now uniformly asked and result in equalizing the interview component of the individual assessment.

Program Improvement

As a result of portfolio assessment, suggestions made by our consultant as well as our constant review, many elements of the program have, we feel, improved. Our program requirements have been revised, we have clarified our objectives and goals and we have expanded our recruitment procedures which has resulted in a 100% increase in the number of our majors. We also realized that the program guidelines needed to be carefully disseminated to the students by means of advisement (upon admission to the program, during registration and following their assessment video taping) and in departmental meetings (twice a year).

Conclusions

One thing we are especially aware of is that assessment is an ongoing process. We will never have "completed" our work with theatre assessment. Our goals are dynamic, our students change and the faculty continues to grow throughout the process. Assessment is a constant re-evaluation of objectives, procedures, methods and materials. It is precisely the kind of challenge which keeps our department current and vital.

The Visual Communications Portfolio: The Measure of One's Work

Martin Holloway and Robin Landa

What is Visual Communications?

Visual Communications as an industry is a direct outgrowth of the communications needs of a literate populace, particularly in a free market economy. It is the application of art and communication skills to the needs of business and industry. These applications include: marketing and selling products and services; creating visual identities for institutions, products, and companies; and visually enhancing messages in publications. The mass communications media -- print, film, and electronic -- are the vehicles for these visual messages. Areas of specialization include advertising, graphic design, illustration, and commercial photography.

The field as it exists today is a melding of the separate disciplines of art, technology and marketing into the hybrid discipline of visual communications. In their "pure" forms, these are often at cross purposes. United, they have the common purpose of communicating concise and persuasive messages through the mass media to a targeted audience -- with a specific objective in mind. Increasingly, artists, designers and art directors are called upon not simply to decorate a communications message, but to participate fully in its rationale, conception and production.

Since visual communications plays a key role in the appearance of almost all print, film, and electronic media, it becomes a primary creator of the visual artifacts of our environment and popular culture. It is an integral component of contemporary society, of the free enterprise system, and of mass culture. Visual communications is a powerful propagator of the vital issues of today; a legitimate aesthetic voice; and an industry employing thousands in New Jersey and across the country. There is great potential for profound contribution to society in the visual communications profession.

The Function of Portfolio Review in the Profession

Historically, portfolio review is the method used by visual communications professionals to measure one's work throughout one's career, from entry through senior positions. In industry, the portfolio is *the* most important credential -- more critical than degrees earned, professional awards, grade point average, or schools attended. In the end, the actual work produced by a visual artist must speak for itself.

The entry-level portfolio should demonstrate the abilities that are needed by fledgling professionals, including visual skills, problem-solving skills, creative skills and technological skills. A professional visual communications portfolio contains roughly the same number of works and demonstrates the same skills, except that the professional portfolio contains production pieces as well as simulated mock-ups. In both instances, for the entry-level as well as the advanced professional, positions are obtained and careers are advanced primarily as a result of the efficacy of the work produced -- as displayed in the portfolio.

Portfolio Review in Design Education

For working professionals, the portfolio primarily demonstrates performance. In education, the portfolio demonstrates performance also, but equally important for the education process, it demonstrates potential. At Kean, portfolio review is used as an evaluation tool for virtually every studio course. In addition, the Fine-Arts Department has identified three critical stages where portfolio review is utilized outside of classroom teaching; first, when a student enters a department as a major; second, when a student applies for the BFA degree program; and third, when a student graduates from the BFA degree program. These reviews are detailed in Figures 1, 2, and 3.

Although certain components of visual communications are skill or knowledge based, the heart of the discipline is creative performance. Since the conventional forms of testing tend to measure acquired knowledge and intellectual skills rather than creative performance, we rely upon the long standing tradition of portfolio review as our primary instrument.

Creativity in visual communications is not measured in absolute terms of right or wrong, but rather by the degrees of success demonstrated in solving problems, applying visual skills, and achieving personal interpretations. The evaluation of creative work is particularly difficult because it defies precise definition and is seen differently by each reviewer. Therefore, we feel that it is essential to use several visual communications faculty members in the process of reviewing student portfolios. Our experience has revealed that consensus is surprisingly easy to achieve.

A college senior's visual communications portfolio contains about twelve to twenty pieces of work. The type of work included in the portfolio depends upon the artist's area of specialization. For example, someone pursuing a career in advertising might have four ad campaigns, each campaign consisting of three related advertisements, and a few single ads in his/her portfolio. A student piece is usually in the form of a comprehensive layout which is a detailed representation of a design. Typography, illustration, photography, paper, color and layout are presented closely enough to the finish product to convey an accurate impression of the printed or constructed piece.

The Kean College Fine Arts Department

The Fine Arts Department of Kean College offers two degree programs: the Bachelor of Arts and the Bachelor of Fine Arts. The B.A., a liberal arts degree, provides the student with an art foundation and a wide range of art electives. This degree is not intended for students who wish to pursue a professional art career, rather it is intended to provide a general background of art knowledge and skills as part of a liberal arts degree. The B.F.A., a professional level degree, allows the career-oriented student to develop the skills and knowledge necessary in preparing for an art career. The B.F.A. programs include Studio Art, Interior Design , and Visual Communications.

The Kean College Visual Communications Program

The mission of the BFA: Visual Communications degree program is to educate the whole person, providing a broad base of knowledge in the liberal arts, in the fine arts, as well as depth in the student's area of specialization. The visual communications professional needs visual and verbal skills; communication skills, writing skills, research skills, as well as the "well-rounded" liberal arts foundation to better ensure the ability to solve a wide variety of practical communication problems. The BFA in Visual Communications provides the student with the educational springboard for a career. The BFA also provides a foundation for graduate study in visual communications. The program offers three areas of specialization. These are advertising, graphic design, and illustration. Our most significant goal is to provide a background of intellectual and creative stimulation as well as professional skills which will enable our graduates to reach their full potential artistically and professionally.

Primary Educational Goals of the B.F.A.: Visual Communications Program

To develop knowledge of and/or expertise in the following:

I.   Fundamentals of Visual Form

    A. Visual Arts Fundamentals

        1. The manipulation of basic visual elements in 2-D and 3-D configurations
        2. Drawing used both as a visualizing tool and as an expressive medium

    B. Art History: Prehistoric through Modern

    C. Visual Arts Elective Experiences

II. Materials, Tools & Technologies

    A. Studio Skills: such as rendering techniques, paste-up and presentation -- with an emphasis on accuracy and craftsmanship

    B. Photographic Skills: picture-taking/developing/printing; graphic arts photography including the copy camera, photostats, color keys, dry transfers, and other similar processes

    C. Computer Skills: use of software for design, drawing, typographic and page layout applications

III. Methodology, Problem Solving, The Creative Process

    A. Methodology: an exploration of the system of methods used in the visual communications industry

    B. Problem solving: how to find visual/verbal solutions to practical communications problems

IV. Visual Communications Applications

    A. Advertising: print and T.V.

    B. Graphic Design: editorial, informational, and promotional

    C. Illustration: advertising and editorial

V.   Professional Practices

    A. The business of visual communications

        1. the client/designer relationship
        2. visual communications as a marketing tool
        3. business practices: soliciting clients, pricing and ethical guidelines, contracts and proposals, legal issues
        4. production for print and electronic media: the process of realizing a project from initial concept through delivery of finished job
        5. professional resources: trade associations, professional literature, exhibits, trade shows, conferences

VI. Theory

    A. The historical, aesthetic, and theoretical foundation for visual communications practice

    B. Seminal figures, schools, movements in the history of art and design

   C. Visual communications in marketing, aesthetic and societal contexts

   D. Changing roles and responsibilities of visual communications

   E. Emerging scholarship and criticism in visual communications

VII. Individual Point of View (The Creative Process)

   The creative leap: synthesis of formal, technical, practical and theoretical components into a personal gestalt and artistic output which addresses both the functional requirements of the project and also the personal aesthetic of the artist

VIII. The Portfolio: A Body of Work

   A. The Portfolio: Preparation of a professional portfolio for entry into the work force in the student's chosen visual communications discipline

   B. The Job Search: Preparing for the job search process, e.g., writing a resume and cover letter, networking, interviewing, developing resources for job opportunities

Portfolio Review Periods in the Fine Arts Department

Entering the Fine Arts Department

Entering Freshman must have a body of work reviewed by the department prior to their being admitted to a degree program. This body of work consists of four exercises prescribed by the department and up to five examples of their work (See Figure 1). This portfolio is reviewed by faculty and determines the student's acceptability to the department as well as identifying those students in need of a remedial drawing course offered by the department.

Entering the BFA Degree Program

Admission to the B.F.A.: Visual Communications degree is dependent upon completion of a minimum of 30 credits in the major, a major grade point average of B (3.0), and faculty approval based upon portfolio review. The portfolio, containing ten to fifteen pieces of work, is submitted to a committee of three Fine Arts professors. The work represents hand skills, thinking skills, and creative skills learned in the Fine Arts foundation courses and in three beginning visual communications courses.

An instrument is used by the committee of reviewers to determine the applicant's acceptability (See Figure 2). The instrument was developed in relation to the B.F.A. program's goals and the experience of the faculty; it formalized what was a previously intuitive process by individual faculty. The instrument has gone through three revisions which were based on its efficacy in the evaluation process. The faculty have a conference to critique the instrument after each review period and it is revised as necessary. The students receive copies of their reviews. We photograph some portfolios as a part of record keeping and as part of our assessment of student learning and development.

Exiting the BFA Degree Program

The exit review conducted to assess student learning in the B.F.A.: Visual Communications is conducted during the senior year in a final course entitled "Portfolio." In this course, the student further develops his/her work with an emphasis on meeting standards of professional competence and focusing individual strengths. The dual purpose of this course -- to develop a presentation method and to produce additional professional level work -- results in a finished portfolio preparing the student for a job search.

Three or four faculty members, including the instructor of the portfolio course, review the senior's portfolio utilizing an assessment instrument (See Figure 3). This review, unlike the review for entrance into the B.F.A., is conducted in front of the student with the student's participation. It is not unlike a job interview. The students receive copies of their written reviews. We photograph senior portfolios as a part of our record keeping and assessment of development.

Figure 1. Portfolio Review. Upon Entrance into the Department as a Major.

PLEASE SUBMIT EXERCISES ONE THROUGH FIVE.
THE SIXTH ITEM, PORTFOLIO, IS OPTIONAL.

SIZE OF WORK IS 12" X 15" AND MUST BE RETURNED, UNFOLDED IN A 12" X 15"
ENVELOPE TO THE ADDRESS GIVEN ABOVE.

<u>EXERCISES</u>

1. Draw a self-portrait using a mirror.

2. Draw an interior scene using shading, perspective, and proportion.

3. On one sheet of paper draw your own hand in three different positions. One
    of these drawings must be exclusively in ball point or felt tip pen.

4. Create a collage by tearing and/or cutting paper, magazines or other two
    dimensional materials. Depict one of the following themes: still life
    compositions, landscape or interior scene.

5. In a hand written statement of approximately two hundred words, give your
    reason for coming to Kean College of New Jersey and studying art.

6. (Optional) Submit a total of five examples of your work. These can be slides
    and/or photographs of any kind of art work: painting, ceramics, photography,
    prints, sculpture. On the back of each photograph write your name, and the
    title, medium and size (HxWxD) on the side it should be viewed if hand held.
    On the other side, print your address and social security number.

Figure 2. Portfolio Review. Upon Application for the BFA Degree Program.

BFA: Visual Communications
Entrance Review

Student's Name: _____

DESIGN

Manipulation of visual elements: 2-D and 3-D media

A   A-   B+   B   B-   C+   C   D   N/A (not applicable)

DRAWING

Visualizing tool. Utilizing elements and principles of design.

A   A-   B+   B   B-   C+   C   D   N/A

MATERIAL AND TOOLS

Exploration of media.

A   A-   B+   B   B-   C+   C   D   N/A

INDIVIDUAL POINT OF VIEW

Evidence of originality in solution to problems.

A   A-   B+   B   B-   C+   C   D   N/A

PRESENTATION AND CRAFTSMANSHIP

A   A-   B+   B   B-   C+   C   D   N/A

COMMENTS:

PROFESSOR'S SIGNATURE _____

Figure 3. Portfolio Review. Upon Graduation from the BFA Degree Program.

<u>BFA: Visual Communications</u>
Exit Review

FUNDAMENTALS OF VISUAL FORM

*   Manipulation of design elements   *   Use of color
              *   Drawing as a visualizing and expressive medium

A   A-   B+   B   B-   C+   C   D   N/A (not applicable)

MATERIALS, TOOLS AND TECHNOLOGIES

*Studio skills   *Photographic skills   *Computer skills   *Craftsmanship

A   A-   B+   B   B-   C+   C   D   N/A

APPLICATIONS

        Content (graphic design, advertising, illustration, media)

A   A-   B+   ·B   B-   C+   C   D   N/A

Comments:

PROFESSIONAL PRACTICES - (Evaluation from written exam)
THEORY - (Evaluation from written exam)

INDIVIDUAL POINT OF VIEW

        Originality in solution to visual problems

A   A-   B+   B   B-   C+   C   D   N/A

PRESENTATION, RESUME & OTHER SELF-PROMOTION

        Selection and organization of information - Design and production quality

A   A-   B+   B   B-   C+   C   D   N/A

Professor's Comments:

Professor's Signature _____

Conclusion

The essential problem is not to evaluate the validity of portfolio review as a general concept; we accept this method of assessing one's abilities as the industry standard. We must evaluate the specific codification of the process as we have developed it. We believe portfolio review is the most reliable instrument in evaluating creative visual work. We use this instrument in concert with many other factors in order to assess student learning and development. These include student surveys, alumni surveys, use of program consultants and advisory boards, student portfolio reviews conducted by professional organizations such as the New York Art Directors Club and the Art Directors Club of New Jersey, awards won by students, and employment statistics.

The Use of Portfolios in an Assessment Model for Undergraduate Elementary Education and K-12 Subject Matter Majors

Janet G. Prince

Students in teacher training programs at Kean College of New Jersey have been gathering materials of their own and ideas of others, logging records of their teaching and learning experiences, and keeping notes from specific teacher education courses for most of the decades since 1855 when the college was founded as a normal school. Recently these collections of materials, now commonly called portfolios, have become important in the assessment process of the teacher education programs at this college.

Overview of the Assessment Model

The assessment model which utilizes the portfolio as an intrinsic component was developed by the Assessment Committee of the Department of Instruction, Curriculum, and Administration. This department houses graduate and undergraduate teacher education programs and educational administration programs. An Assessment Committee developed an outcomes assessment and has for the past few years used the model to assess undergraduate teacher education programs, specifically the Elementary Education Program and the Kindergarten through Grade 12 Subject Matter Specialization (in the academic areas of science, social studies, mathematics, and English) Program.

The underlying premise of the formalized assessment process or model is that successful teachers reflect on their teaching, on their decisions, on their problems and solutions to those problems, on their students, and on the processes of teaching and learning. The decision to use the portfolio as the centerpiece of the assessment model came about after careful examination of what teachers do and what could be evaluated.

The model includes three components: (1) Portfolio; (2) Written Self Study; and (3) Exit Interview. This threefold process is not unlike the model used by accrediting agencies, such as the National Council for the Accreditation of Teacher Education (NCATE) and various other regional accrediting agencies that evaluate institutions and college and university programs of study. These components are similar to those undertaken for accrediting agencies where institutions first write self studies and then submit portfolio-type collections of data and materials that support their self studies and bids for accreditation. Visitations to the institutions by accrediting agencies correspond in many ways to the Exit Interview component of this assessment model.

Each Elementary Education Major or K-12 Subject Matter Major at Kean College of New Jersey is required to compile a portfolio. The purposes of the portfolio are to provide documentation for the student's Written Self Study; to develop an organized resource for future teaching; and to produce a documented record of professional experiences that might be used as an expanded resume. By using videotapes that might be part of the portfolio, a potential employer can see and hear a sample of the professional intern's teaching without leaving his/her office.   This portfolio is a collection of documents and objects from all professional education courses and professional field experiences in the student's education program.   These documents and objects may be lesson plans, evaluations of teaching or performances, judged and graded assignments, curriculum units, learning centers, samples of testing or assessment materials, videotapes and audiotapes of teaching, logs kept for the three field experiences, samples of writing including those with revisions and especially samples of writing from writing emphasis courses, photographs of exhibits or special events undertaken by the student, written evaluations or critiques by the college supervisor or cooperating teacher of the student's teaching done during the professional internship, a transcript of the student's college record, a copy of the student's educational program, and other documents that are pertinent to the student's professional growth and development.

The Written Self Study is a document written by the student as he/she completes the professional internship. The student is asked to respond to certain statements or questions that require descriptions of experiences, evidence of the understanding of the process of teaching, documentation, and evaluation of these experiences that he/she has had in college-based courses and field experiences. The Written Self Study provides a narrative concerning what, where, when, how, and under what conditions a specific experience has been undergone. It also provides written evidence of the student's reflection about his or her pre-professional teaching experiences, a self evaluation of that teaching, descriptions of how certain concepts may have been taught differently, narratives on how aspects of classroom management may have been altered, and statements on how teaching experiences may have changed the student's views about the process of teaching and the profession of teaching.

The Exit Interview involves the examination of the Portfolio and Written Self Study. During the Exit Interview the student is engaged by the interviewer in discussions that elicit evaluative and reflective thinking. The interviewer asks about specific experiences that the student has had in teaching, what the experiences meant, whether the meaning of the experience could be interpreted differently, whether the experience went well or not, whether the student could have altered the outcome of the experience. The interviewer looks for evidence of a questioning frame of mind on the part of the student.

The assessment model devised for Elementary Education and K-Grade 12 Subject Matter Education Majors involves the cognitive processes of application of knowledge, analysis, creativity, and judgment or evaluation from the exiting student who is becoming a teacher. The model involves examination by the student of his/her own performance as a teacher. The portfolio provides the student's documentation of his/her experiences. The Self Study and Exit Interview provide the media for reflection: reflection by the student about his/her teaching experience, reflection about the process of teaching, reflection about learning, and reflection about his/her role in the improvement or alteration of that teaching process. The three components of the assessment model are interrelated. The Portfolio serves as the proof of the experience, and the Written Self Study and Exit Interview give expression to the contents of that portfolio.

Definition of the Portfolio

Although the portfolio has long been a requirement of student teaching or professional internship courses, it was usually limited to materials collected during the internship. Redefinition of the portfolio was necessary when the portfolio became a part of the assessment process. For purposes of assessment, the portfolio includes materials from all three field experiences and all professional courses. These materials may include logs of observations of teaching, lesson plans, mini-course or unit outlines, graded/judged papers, community studies, ideas gathered from the work of master teachers, teacher-made games, ideas for activities, and descriptions of special teaching techniques observed. The portfolio may fit into a large carton or in several boxes or cartons, a large barrel, and may be kept in a garage or in a dry basement. Whatever container is used, the professional intern's portfolio tends to be a somewhat untidy amalgam of many things useful or potentially useful to the teacher.

The student starts his/her portfolio during the first of three field courses he/she is required to take in the undergraduate teacher education major. The three field courses include an introductory field experience course (3 s. h.) where students visit urban and suburban school districts; a junior field experience course (2 s. h.) where the student visits the same school one day a week for an entire semester and where some teaching is done; and the professional internship (10 s. h.) where the student is assigned to a classroom in a school for an entire semester or fifteen weeks. The content of the portfolio should also reflect the content of fifteen semester hours of on-campus course work which involves studies of measurement, teaching strategies, and motivation; methods of teaching reading and language arts; methods of teaching social studies; methods of teaching science and mathematics; teaching methodologies for teaching specific subject matter areas for K-12 subject matter education majors; and other topics deemed necessary for the education of teachers.

Storage of the portfolio is the student's responsibility, even though it figures importantly in the assessment process. Because the portfolio is literally the student's kit of tools and resources, the portfolio is appropriately left in each student's possession.

The decision about the size of the Portfolio is up to the individual student's needs and vision. Some students are more sensitive to their future needs than others and thus amass large collections of materials. Other students have spare and carefully selected collections of materials. Others collect materials for teaching in many situations. Others concentrate on one grade and on the materials needed for that grade. The most important quality of the portfolio is its usefulness to the student.

The time frame governing the portfolio runs from the initial introductory and exploratory field experience course through the student's completion of the professional internship. The Elementary Education Major Program contains thirty semester hours and the K-12 Subject Matter Area Programs somewhat less. However, because each field experience course must be taken in different semesters, a minimum of three semesters is required to complete each professional education program and, in turn, the portfolio.

Communication with Students

The Assessment Committee of the Department of Instruction, Curriculum, and Administration which houses the Elementary Education Program and the K-12 Subject Matter Program has prepared two small brochures (one for each program) which describe the assessment model and importance of student portfolios in the process. These brochures are given to the faculty members teaching the initial field experience courses and they are, in turn, distributed to the students in those courses. The brochure emphasizes the necessity of keeping a portfolio that may be expanded with each new professional course or field experience taken as part of each teacher education program. The importance of the portfolio as a component of the assessment process is also stressed.

Because transfer students often are given credit for the sophomore field course, they have not in the past received the brochure describing the assessment process and the information regarding the necessity of developing a portfolio. Brochures are now sent to all students when they are informed of their acceptance into the Elementary Education Program or the K-12 Subject Matter Specialization Program.

Examination of the Portfolio

Prior to the examination of the Portfolio and the Exit Interview, the student is required to complete a Written Self Study. The Written Self Study consists of a minimum of two questions to be answered by the student in good essay form. The questions are designed to elicit reflection from the student on the teaching process, learning, motivation of youngsters, progress of children, classroom management, the profession of teaching, and other topics related to the teaching-learning process.

Examples of questions are:

Describe, document, and reflect on the variety of different strategies that you have designed and used in instruction, and document the variety of written, audio-visual, and tactile materials you have used in the teaching-learning process.

Describe and reflect on the experiences you have had with respect to the variety of cultural, social, economic, and learning characteristics of students and how those varying characteristics influenced the learning process. Document your reflections with specific examples.

Describe the theories of learning and motivation and the teaching approaches that you drew upon as you taught and interacted with the children in this classroom and school setting.

The Written Self Study is one sample of the student's reflections about the processes of teaching and learning and the myriad components of each. It is also assumed that the Exit Interview and the subsequent examination of the portfolio will also exhibit reflection on the part of the professional intern. The Written Self Study provides the first piece of evidence of a student's reflectivity in the assessment.

The Exit Interview is utilized to determine whether the student can in an interview setting demonstrate reflective thinking about the processes of teaching and learning. The Exit Interview is centered around the examination of the professional intern's portfolio, and the interviewer poses questions about the contents of the portfolio that evoke reflectivity from the student about his/her teaching experiences.

Questions asked of the professional intern as he/she completes his/her internship focus on the lesson that the student perceives as his/her best or most successful.

These questions are:

Describe the best and most successful lesson that you have taught. Find the lesson plan for that lesson in your Portfolio.

Why do you feel that this was your best lesson? What teaching strategy did you use? What devices or techniques did you use to get feedback from the students which informed you that they understood the content of the lesson? What opening set did you use? How did you close the lesson?

What did you learn about your pupils from teaching this lesson?
What did you learn about teaching from your success with this lesson?
What would you have done differently?

Conversely, the interviewer also asks the intern to identify the poorest or least successful lesson he/she taught. Questions are:

Why do you rate this lesson your poorest or least successful?

Can you tell specifically or in what component of the lesson did it go astray?

If you taught this lesson again what changes would you make?

If you had the opportunity to reteach the same content of this lesson, how would you teach the material?

Since professional interns often have difficulty with classroom management, the supervisor also asks some of the following questions concerning this area of teaching:

What were your most difficult moments as you took over your class for a whole day?

What strategies did the cooperating teacher use to maintain cooperation of the students and order in the classroom? What methods did the cooperating teacher use to enable students to develop self discipline?

How did you manage the class when various children left the room for special classes or activities?

How did you know when you had the confidence of the youngsters in your class and also know that you had control of the situation?

What are the most important points you learned in your professional internship about classroom management and discipline?

Other areas of teaching are explored, such as mainstreaming, multicultural relations in the classroom, motivation of children, viable learning theories,and the student's developing philosophy of education. The professional intern's lesson plans, written logs of observations and other materials designed, used, and collected by the student are exhibited and discussed during the Exit Interview.

Rating of the Portfolio

Thus far, portfolios that have been examined have not been graded, rated, or scored. The Assessment Committee does not intend to rate the worth of each student's portfolio at this point in the development of the assessment model. Because of the personal and subjective nature of a portfolio, and because a collection of materials is often based upon what the individual perceives as important to him/her, it would seem that rating a portfolio of this type would not be particularly fruitful. Unlike portfolios of artists or writers, the teacher's portfolio has purposes other than meeting certain universally accepted artistic criteria. The portfolio of a professional intern can provide a view of the individual as a teacher, but the variety of materials collected by that individual is only important when the portfolio is accompanied by an explanation of its contents.

A holistic scoring system has been applied to rate the student's Written Self Study. This system employs a three-point scale with three points indicating a high degree of "professional growth and reflection"; two points indicating a moderate degree of "professional growth and reflection"; and one point indicating a minimal degree of "professional growth and reflection. The Exit Interviews will also be rated holistically with the same scale after a greater number of professional interns are interviewed.

Evaluation of the Use of the Portfolio in the Assessment Process

Studies in the use of this assessment model have gone on since 1989. Results have indicated that as students discussed and exhibited their portfolios they did indeed reflect on the teaching experiences they had in their professional internships. They revealed awareness of the pupils' idiosyncrasies and learning problems. They produced effective lesson plans and often talked knowledgeably about improving the delivery of those lessons. Some exhibited scholarship in graded papers. Many showed creativity in their approach to teaching through their projects and activities designed for their students. They often exhibited enthusiasm for their own pupils and the teaching and learning processes.

On the less positive side, members of the Assessment Committee who rated the Written Self Studies and examined the portfolios and conducted the interviews were concerned that students were sometimes unable to engage in analytical or critical thinking with respect to their own teaching. Of particular concern were the problems students had in making connections between theory and practice. Students also seemed to be overly dependent on prescriptions rather than on viable pedagogical theories. Students often expressed oversimplified views of what it means to teach. Further, the portfolio and interview did not always reveal how students interact with children, professional peers, parents, community members, administrators, or supervisors. Interviewers often found that the professional interns were very defensive about their experiences. Interns found it very hard to be critical of themselves or to admit to poorly taught lessons. This seemed to be a characteristic of those interns who were unsure of themselves or who had trouble with students in their classes or with the process of teaching during the professional internship.

Even with its drawbacks, the portfolio appears to be useful as a tool for the assessment of teacher training programs, especially when it is used in tandem with the Written Self Study and Exit Interview. Two reasons for an outcomes assessment plan are: (1) to find out how well a student is learning; and (2) to determine whether a program or curriculum is an effective one. The results of the Written Self Studies and the Exit Interviews in conjunction with the examination of each portfolio clearly indicate where the teacher training programs can be improved, such as in the need to improve the teaching of pedagogical theories and to improve the connections between theories and practice. A general picture of how well a student is doing in the program is also evident. Although the assessment model does not directly reveal the quality of the interpersonal skills of the intern, the student often inadvertently relates information about interpersonal matters within the interview situation. It is often the content of the portfolio which prompts the discussion.

Within the next year or two the assessment process will be made an intrinsic part of the undergraduate teacher training programs. Each supervisor of each intern will be charged with administering the Written Self Study to the professional intern, examining the Portfolio, and conducting the Exit Interview. With this in place, more information will be available to assess the teacher education programs and accomplishments of the individual students in those programs. Serendipitously, more information will be available to judge the assessment process in which the portfolio plays a most important part.

Portfolio Assessment of the Nursing Program

Virginia M. Fitzsimons and Dula F. Pacquiao

Introduction

The initial focus of the Portfolio Assessment of the Department of Nursing is an examination of the program objectives of the curriculum. Level objectives were analyzed to determine continuity of curricular themes in bringing to fruition the terminal objectives of the program.

On our first approach at Portfolio Assessment the faculty attempted to include all nine program objectives in the review. They quickly learned that this was far too broad a sweep of the program to see measurable outcomes. It was simply too cumbersome a task to consider so much material. But, the value of finding this one initial "outcome" was that it forced the faculty to prioritize the objectives. In the beginning, the faculty said, "These are all important, we can't choose one over other." However, when pressed they did, and without too much difficulty, identify the Nursing Process as a fundamental framework upon which the other objectives, and thus the entire program, was built.

Nursing Process is by other names, the scientific method, critical thinking, decision making or problem solving. Its component parts are: assessment, planning, implementation and evaluation. It is a systematic, science-based, inferential and standardized method of defining the nursing needs of clients in diverse settings of care. The Nursing Process is the single common framework used by the American Nurses' Association in setting Standards of Care for all areas of clinical nursing practice. The nomenclature is known and accepted by professional nurses internationally.

In the Department of Nursing, the term client, refers to a family or individual, sick or well, at home, in a hospital or in the community at large. In each of the four clinical nursing courses, a Nursing Process Record (NPR) is completed by the student. This documentation records the application of the theoretical and scientific knowledge used by the nurse in the actual delivery of the nursing service to the client. The NPR is a vehicle used to describe the context of the care giving situation, bringing together the empirical and intuitive aspects of thinking inherent in formulating highly individualized care. This NPR is analogous to the clinical documentation (nurses notes) recognized as the legal standard in all clinical agencies.

In an era of greater demands for quality nursing service and limited resources, employers and third party reimbursers demand accountability and specificity in the care delivered. And the one method they use to determine that quality of care is the documentation of the Nursing Process. The centrality of care outcomes achievement in defining effectiveness of care given predominate every facet of nursing practice. Expectations by both consumer and providers of healthcare for high level proficiency of nursing graduates in deliberating appropriate parameters of effective care and documenting progress toward their achievement exist.

Educators are also grappling with defining and identifying descriptors of baccalaureate levels of care (versus technical level care). Although the need for higher education is recognized as essential in today's nursing practice, educational programs have failed to provide proof of the distinct attributes of their graduates. The ambiguity in the products of the three programs for entry to nursing practice remains.

Discussion

Currently, there are three levels which stratify the Nursing curriculum. Level I consists of entry behaviors expected of incoming Nursing Majors. These were identified in order to set a data base on the ability to use the Nursing Process. These are the same behaviors recognized as minimum exit criteria for associate degree graduates by the National League for Nursing, the accreditation body of nursing programs across the country. These criteria state that the associate degree graduate can give nursing care to the individual, in an acute care setting using standard nursing protocols, in commonly occurring situations and implementing a professionally developed plan of teaching health care information. The Department of Nursing, requires the entering Nursing Major to demonstrate competency at this level by completing the Simulated Clinical Examination. This Simulated Clinical NPR constitutes the first part of the students' Portfolio Assessment Packet.

Level II moves the students through courses developed to expand their practice scope to include well families in the community, comprehensive health appraisals of individual family members, and an introduction to community assessment. Introduced also in Level II are the conceptual models basic to Professional Nursing, current issues and trends in health care and teaching/learning principles. The culmination of this level is the NPR done in NURS 3100 with family focus and psycho-social emphasis. This NPR becomes the second component of the students' Portfolio Assessment Packet.

Level III address the family in crisis, the family with a member who is chronically ill and such concepts as leadership, quality assurance, change theory, group process and advanced communication skills. Students select appropriate conceptual models to guide their application of nursing practice and all of these things are structured within the framework of the Nursing Process. Three NPRs result from Level III. One is developed as part of NURS 4000, another is a product of NURS 4100 and the last one is accomplished through an independent practicum in NURS 4900. It is expected that each student can demonstrate all nine program objectives on the NURS 4900 project. These three NPRs are the final component parts of the Portfolio.

In addition to the NPRs in the three levels, a survey of employers of the graduates was done to help identify the characteristic documentation which emerged. Descriptors used by employers were ambiguous and non-specific. The need to develop a more focused questionnaire to complement the open-ended questionnaire used has been identified by the faculty.

It is envisioned that the initial impetus of Portfolio Assessment will be largely faculty-directed until further development of descriptors of student documentation at the baccalaureate level are identified and translated into a tool for measuring program outcomes through the three level NPRs. Plans for increased involvement by the alumni and Nursing Majors in the NURS 4900 course are explored in order to maximize the number of portfolios in the sample, thus increasing the samples from which generalizations are drawn. Another advantage of this proposal lies in the opportunity for realizing several viewpoints in data interpretation which are critical in triangulation of data to insure validity and reliability of method used. Confidentiality of student files will be a major consideration before individual portfolios are opened to Nursing Majors and alumni. At present, a broad range of students representing the top and low group have been targeted in order to maximize the range of descriptors identified.

Individual student portfolios are kept in distinct (color coded) packets which are integrated in their files in the Department. The Department upholds the philosophy that individual students should have free access to their files and share the responsibility in updating data necessary for their professional development throughout the program. Each student therefore is delegated the primary responsibility to update his/her portfolio reflecting congruence with the departmental philosophy.

The central role of student and alumni participation in the process has been presented by the faculty and the Chairperson, underlining as its primary goal of the process as evaluation of the program and not the student. An atmosphere of genuine openness by faculty to positive or negative results has been established at the outset.

Information generated from Portfolio Assessment is kept in the Departmental file. Significant findings are shared with both students and alumni so that ongoing feedback about the process and the program are obtained. In other words, Portfolio Assessments are viewed as integral components of formative and summative evaluative processes of program outcomes. Salient findings will be used in curriculum planning and evaluation as well as in developing extra curricular activities in the program.

Portfolio Assessments in the Department of Nursing is in its formative stage. A qualitative approach in generating data inductively has been chosen to formulate à compendium of descriptors of students' documentation of nursing care with the goal of delineating the language and behaviors of baccalaureate level of nursing practice. Parameters of professional nursing practice through baccalaureate education will be comprehensively identified through this approach. Once a pattern of language and behaviors are evident, a quantitative methodology will be used hand in hand to deductively assess the achievement of program outcomes.

The faculty firmly believe in the necessity for assessing both the quality and effectiveness of nursing practice. This belief is rooted in the philosophy that nursing is a delicate balance between the scientific and the artful way of dealing with human beings. Hence, a comprehensive assessment of program outcomes require a combination of both qualitative and quantitative data collection methodologies. The evolution of a quantitative measuring tool will be a faculty project in conjunction with the College-wide effort similarly directed to its development.

Reliability of findings can be assured in a variety of ways. Descriptive criteria drawn from Portfolio Assessments can be examined by reputable members of the profession representing both education and practice arenas of nursing. Criteria can also be piloted by other upper division baccalaureate programs of nursing. Similarly, increasing the number of samples of portfolio assessments will enhance reliability. Dissemination of study protocols and its methodology will allow replication by others using comparable conditions.

Measures toward reliability are at the same time ways of enhancing validity of findings. In addition to the ones previously stated, a large, randomized sample minimizes chance occurrence of findings. Descriptive criteria can be categorized in terms of how they reflect individual program objectives. Again, consultation with a cadre of qualified members of nursing practice and education should be sought to determine their relevance and adequacy. Triangulation of data obtained from both quantitative and qualitative means will strengthen the validity of the findings.

Participation by students and alumni in portfolio assessments provide data relevant to the existing program and effects of changes overtime delineating the program outcomes' responsiveness to current trends in nursing and its relevance to long term professional development. It is ideal to do a longitudinal as well as cross-sectional sampling of portfolio assessments. At the present time, a longitudinal assessment has been started for students within the program with the goal of follow-up after graduation. However, the graduate questionnaire and feedback from employers are the best data source for the longitudinal influence of the program objectives at the present time. Portfolio assessment therefore is an ongoing, longitudinal study of program outcomes with rich ramifications in curricular development and evaluation. Presumably, effects of significant changes such as those emanating from the curriculum, student demography, and professional nursing practice arena may be reflected through Portfolio Assessment.

Findings from Portfolio Assessments can have considerable influence in curriculum development, program marketing, staff development and budgetary allocations. Parameters of baccalaureate level of nursing practice can be more adequately described, paving the way for differentiating baccalaureate prepared nurses from other graduates. In nursing with its three-tiered entry requirements to practice, these data will create significant debate and soul searching. The possibility of evolving differential licensure requirements and delineating suitable practice arenas for baccalaureate graduates may be in sight.

Because of the potential impact of Portfolio Assessment on the program and upon the nursing profession in general, a cautious approach toward data analysis and its application should balance the exhilaration and excitement of its findings. At the inception of the project, faculty must clarify their beliefs and values regarding the process itself, its purpose, methodology and use of its findings. A healthy perspective can be maintained in that, its findings are relevant in terms of diagnosing program weaknesses and celebrating its strengths. For faculty to share this viewpoint requires assurance from administration that they too are committed to the same purposes of Portfolio Assessments.

<u>**Pilot Study Review of Qualitative Data**
of Nursing Majors' Outcomes Assessment Portfolios</u>

<u>**Data Source**</u>   N=5

Transcription of Notes:

LEVEL I - Document analyzed: Simulated Clinical Examination

This tool is used to measure the competency of the Nursing Major candidate in utilizing the Nursing Process at the level of the exit criteria for Associate Degree graduates as stated by the Council of Associate Degree Programs of the National League for Nursing. The upper division curriculum is grounded in the assumptions that Levels II and III are building upon these exit competencies of Level I.

Particular emphasis continues to be on the process and use of the Nursing Process.

Assessment

Diagnostic statements not consistent with NANDA
Highly focused on the individual
Little assessment reflecting family
Predominantly physical/technical problems identified

Planning

> Distinguished short from long term goals
> Prioritized appropriately nursing diagnoses

Implementation

> Actions nurse directed
> The locus of control is with the nurse
> Very minimal family involvement
> Focus on the individual
> Actions highly technical/physical

Evaluation

> Expected outcomes stated in technical/physical parameters

Assessor's Reflections

Specific structure for use of nursing process appear to be useful for the students to complete the simulated clinical. Faculty are pursuing computerization of simulated clinical exams using the language and format of NANDA.

> Technical competency evident throughout
> Knowledge of stress theory vocabulary

> Minimal psychosocial assessment however, it is appropriate for technical level preparation.

LEVEL II - Document Analyzed: Well Family Nursing Process Record
        NURS 3100 - Professional Nursing Practice With the Well Family

This tool is used to measure the competency of the student in utilizing the Nursing Process at Level II in the curriculum.

This course is taken in the Spring semester of the Junior year. Prerequisites include admission to the Nursing Department, NURS 3000 and Physics 1001.

Course emphases include: use of the Nursing Process reflecting continued study of nursing models and their application in clinical practice, comprehensive health assessment of the individual, family and community, culminating in a Nursing Process Record addressing teaching/learning needs of the family based on an assessed health risk(s).

Assessment

        Focus on family assessment
        Identification of strengths/limitations
        Socio-cultural
        Developmental
        Health maintenance beliefs and practices
        Social class status
        Value orientations
        Interactional patterns
        Decision making patterns

Community Assessment

        Immediate neighborhood
        Access and use of resources

Tools Used

    Physical Examination
    Nutritional Assessment
    Genogram
    Attachment Index
    Network Analysis

Language of Nursing Theory Used

    Orem
    Newman
    Henderson

Language of Other Theory Bases Used

    Duvall (family developmental stages)

Collaborative Assessment Reflecting Family Perceptions

    Family roles
    Family health beliefs
    Sense of priorities
    Identified needs
    Religious practices
    Safety behaviors
    Developmental task goals

Planning

    Can identify potential problems
    Although nursing diagnosis is individually focused, family orientation is
        consistently evident
    Emphasis on teaching/learning needs

Implementation

> Client directed
> Locus of control is with the family
> Collaborative nursing interventions
> Use referrals to community resources

Evaluation

> Client behavioral indicators used for outcome criteria (rather than
>   physical/laboratory values)
> Outcome identified in collaborative language
> Distinctly identified own personal learning objectives
> Distinctly distinguished personal from professional learning

Assessors' Reflections

> Strong psycho-social emphasis
> Holistic assessment evident
> Focus is on health promotion and wellness
> Teaching role developed
> Movement from concrete thinking to a more abstract level

LEVEL III - Document Analyzed: Family in Crisis
                                 Nursing Process Record
     NURS 4000 Professional Nursing Practice with the Family in Crisis

     This tool is used to measure the competency of the student in utilizing the Nursing Process at Level III in the curriculum.

     This course is taken in the Fall semester of the Senior year. Pre-requisites include NURS 3100, NURS 3300, PSY 3110, and SOC 2100 with pre- or co-requisites of NURS 3900 and MGT SCI 3030.

     Course emphases include: application of systems theory as a basis for health team collaboration and client advocacy, application of Nursing Process in formulating interventions for families in crisis, and development of clinical leadership skills. Special emphasis placed on the planning and evaluation phases of the Nursing Process.

Assessment

          Focus on clients perceptions, feelings and value orientation
          Psycho-social emphasis
          Family assessed as a support system
          Analytical approach to family assessment
          Selective application of nursing theory
          Selective application of crisis theory
          Collaborative assessment with client, family and nursing staff

Planning

          Nursing diagnosis supported by behavioral and psycho-social indicators
          Distinguish between short and long term goals
          Goals are client/family oriented

Implementation

    Family involvement evident
    Locus of control in the collaborative mode
    Actions tend to be rehabilitative (counseling vis a vis administering)
    Appropriate use of referrals (interdisciplinary team or outside community
        resources)

Evaluation

    Behavioral and psycho-social indicators of achievement of outcomes
    Analysis of appropriateness of nursing model to crisis situations

Assessors' Reflections

    Increased repertoire of psycho-social/behavioral indicators used in
        assessment
    Rich and more specific descriptions of psycho-social problems reflecting
        individualized assessment (powerlessness vis a vis alteration in
        coping)
    Distinguished personal from professional learning
    Nursing Process is integrative of nursing theory, crisis theory with finesse
        and fluidity of application
    Students identified difficulty in initiating psycho-social interaction
        independent of physical care
    Inconsistencies in individual clinical faculty expectations evident in
        students' documentation

Summary

    Portfolio Assessment has identified data relevant to documentation of how Level Objectives facilitate the achievement of Program Objectives.

    It has provided information regarding the effectiveness of the curricular plan in directing achievement of Program Objectives. It has been an avenue in assessing the internal validity of the curriculum. Also, it has offered a mechanism for examining consistency in the implementation of the curriculum plan. It has yielded information into curriculum reliability which heretofore was unavailable in standard program evaluation measurements.

This Portfolio Assessment process has raised our level of awareness of program accountability. This is critical in an upper division curriculum, in particular, because we are bridging the gap between technical and professional practice in the most fundamental manner.

Assessment of the individual and collective Portfolios was an experience in witnessing the evolution of student maturation and sophistication in the delivery of Professional Nursing Care. These students actually demonstrated movement from a position of rendering care to an individual, in a routine situation, using standard protocols for care to the more advanced level of family focused and theory based care. By the third level, students were able to document practice suited to a broad range of settings characterized by increased diversity, complexity and extending the which were diverse, more complex and extending the scope of practice from traditional acute care facilities into the community and non-traditional arenas.

Portfolio Assessment in Occupational Therapy

Paula Kramer and Karen Stern

The concept of a portfolio is most common in art or music. However, it can be adapted to other professions as well. As Occupational therapy is a practice profession, it also lends itself to the use of portfolio assessment. The Occupational Therapy Program at Kean College is a baccalaureate program designed to prepare students as entry level occupational therapists. This demands both academic and clinical competencies. As academic performance is measured through various course assignments, there is the need to develop a method for assessing the student's emerging clinical competence. To achieve this, the decision was made to assess the students' clinical performance at several points in the program. This allows us to determine whether the students are meeting the behavioral objectives of the program as they progress through each stage of professional development, in the process creating a portfolio of the student's performance.

In the Kean College Occupational Therapy Program, students are required to participate in three levels of clinical fieldwork, each demanding an increase in clinical competency. Each of these fieldwork levels is in conjunction with a specific course and successful completion of the fieldwork is imperative for successful completion of the course. There are specific objectives for each level and the student must meet these objectives in order to pass the course.

The first fieldwork experience takes place in the pre-professional phase of the program. While students are enrolled in Introduction to Occupational Therapy, they are required to complete 21 hours of volunteer work in an Occupational Therapy department under the supervision of a registered occupational therapist or certified occupational therapy assistant. The objectives for this experience are for the student to gain a beginning understanding of the profession of occupational therapy, to develop a basic comprehension of the scope of the profession, to begin to feel comfortable with patients in a clinical setting, and to demonstrate basic professional behaviors.

An evaluation form was developed to measure these basic competencies. This form is completed by the student's supervisor on completion of the 21 hours of volunteer experience. In addition to rating the student's ability to meet the objectives of the fieldwork experience, supervisors are requested to comment on the student's potential for the profession. The clinical supervisor and the student review the form together and each sign it to acknowledge their agreement with the evaluation. The completed form is placed in the student's departmental file and is the first document of the clinical portfolio.

The next level of fieldwork takes place in the professional phase of the occupational therapy program, during the senior year. There are three fieldwork experiences at this level, one in each of three practice areas: physical dysfunction, psychosocial dysfunction, and pediatrics. These experiences are part of three senior seminar courses, one in each of these practice areas. There are both primary and secondary objectives identified for this level of fieldwork. The primary objectives include the ability to: feel comfortable in the clinical setting, integrate academic learning with clinical practice, utilize supervision effectively and demonstrate professional behavior. Secondary objectives identify specific clinical competencies it is expected the student will develop (i.e. administering evaluations and recording the evaluative data).

Again, an evaluation form was developed for this level of fieldwork, with the same form being used for each of these experiences. The form was designed to measure the student's mastery of the objectives of the course and clinical experience. Clinical supervisors are asked to comment on the student's strengths and limitations in the clinical setting and to indicate the student's readiness for the Level II fieldwork experience.   The student's evaluation for each of these experiences becomes a part of his/her file, expanding the portfolio and providing a picture of the student's emerging competence in the clinical arena.

The third and last level of fieldwork experience is compromised of two three month full time experiences, which follows the completion of all academic coursework. Upon successful completion of the Level II fieldwork experience, the student should demonstrate the following: ability to identify those patients for whom Occupational Therapy is a necessary service; evaluation of the patient's level of functioning, planning and implementation of a treatment program, appropriate termination of treatment, communicating effectively with patients and staff, demonstrate administrative skills, engage effectively in the supervisory process, demonstrate professional behaviors and involvement. The evaluation form used for this experience is one that has been developed by the American Occupational Therapy Association and is used by all accredited occupational therapy programs. For each skill area assessed, the student is evaluated in three domains, performance, attitude and judgement. Each clinical setting develops behavioral objectives for each skill/area of performance assessed. This enhances objectivity for evaluating the student, as well as providing the student with specific information about the expectations for their performance. On completion of these experiences, the student is expected to have the competencies of an entry level therapist and should be prepared to begin clinical work.

A review of the student's portfolio provides a look at his/her development from fledgling student through entry-level therapist. Areas of strength and limitations are identified throughout the student's academic career in terms of clinical performance. By reviewing these fieldwork evaluations sequentially, one is able to see how the student has met the objectives at each level, allowing him/her to progress to the next level, and become an entry level clinician.

FIELDWORK OBJECTIVES FOR INTRODUCTION TO OCCUPATIONAL THERAPY

Participation in the 21 hour (minimum) fieldwork experience will help the student correlate classroom and clinical experiences to be able to:

1. Develop awareness of the organizational structure of the health care facility and its Occupational Therapy Department.

2. Identify and understand the roles and functions of the OTR, COTA, and OTA within the Occupational Therapy Department in a clinical setting.

3. Identify the role of the Occupational Therapist within the health care team.

4. Develop observation skills by observing a patient in as much of the O.T. evaluation - treatment- discharge process as feasible.

5. Understand an overall view of the rehabilitation process and the role of the Occupational Therapist within the process.

6. Identify the types of dysfunction commonly treated by occupational therapists in a clinical setting.

7. Describe the significance of activities used in the O.T. treatment process.

8. Discuss the impact of dysfunction on an individual's performance, as it relates to the health and wellness continuum.

9.   Demonstrate an understanding of the Occupational Therapy process and patient interaction through observational logs and an integration of course material.

10.   Develop an understanding of medical terminology utilized in a clinical setting.

(See Appendix A, Evaluation Form)

OBJECTIVES FOR FIELDWORK EXPERIENCE (LEVEL I): PSYCHOSOCIAL DYSFUNCTION SETTING

In this fieldwork placement, the student will be given a series of tasks and assignments which is coordinated as closely as possible with objectives for both the course and the fieldwork experience, as well as with classroom instruction and assignments.

PRIMARY OBJECTIVES: Upon completion of the Level I fieldwork experience, the student will be able to:

A.   Feel comfortable in a psychosocial dysfunction setting.

B.   Increase his/her own self-awareness in relation to reactions caused by exposure to psychosocial dysfunctions.

C.   Integrate academic learning with clinical practice.

D.   Utilize supervision as a resource for developing problem-solving abilities, communication skills, increasing self-awareness and interpersonal skills and applying theoretical knowledge and concepts.

E.   Demonstrate a level of professional maturity by:

1.   working with persons of various ages and social and ethnic groups, and

2.   recognizing patients'/clients' right to confidentiality.

SECONDARY OBJECTIVES: Upon completion of Level I fieldwork experience, the student will demonstrate skill in:

A.   observation by collecting and recording appropriate observational data throughout the treatment process.

B.   interpersonal relationships by establishing and maintaining rapport with patients/clients and staff.

C.   interviewing by eliciting pertinent information from both patients/clients and staff.

D.   data collection relevant to the patient/client through the use of medical texts, medical charts, interviews with patient/client and staff, observation of the patient/client, evaluative tools/procedures, and other pertinent methods.

E.   administering evaluations and recording the evaluative data.

G.   adapting evaluative tools/procedures when the use of standard/recommended procedures is not possible.

H.   analyzing the impact of the clinical condition upon the patient's/client's occupational performance and performance components.

I.   intervention planning by developing reasonable and realistic plans for intervention.

J.   implement intervention by selecting, using, and adapting therapeutic activities and by structuring the environment to help the patient/client achieve optimal function.

K.   planning and leading a patient/client activity group.

L.   develop an awareness of the community served by the clerkship facility and the community resources available.

(See Appendix B, Evaluation Form)

APPENDIX A

<u>PRE-OCCUPATIONAL THERAPY STUDENT EVALUATION FORM</u>

_____   O.T. 2400   Introduction to Occupational Therapy

_____   Fall   _____   Spring   19 _____

Student _____ Supervisor _____

Facility _____

Dates of Pre-Clinical Experience _____

Total Hours Completed _____

INSTRUCTIONS FOR SUPERVISOR: This evaluation provides important feedback for the student and the instructor. Your rating will be converted to a letter grade and will count 10% of the student's final grade in the Introduction to Occupational Therapy Course.

<u>Please rate this student within the context of an Observational Fieldwork experience.</u>

Please check each item using the following rating scale:

Unsatisfactory   Given 6 opportunities, the student displayed this behavior 2 times or less.

Satisfactory   Given 6 opportunities, the student displayed this behavior 3 or 4 times.

Excellent   Given 6 opportunities, the student displayed this behavior 5 or 6 times.

Not applicable

Please return this form to: Occupational Therapy Department
                               Kean College of New Jersey
                               Morris Avenue
                               Union, N.J.   07083

Developed by **Paula Kramer and Rebecca Dutton**

THE STUDENT DEMONSTRATES

UNSAT. SATIS. EXCELLENT

A: SELF AWARENESS

	UNSAT.	SATIS.	EXCELLENT
1. Is able to recognize and discuss his/her own feelings, attitudes and behavior when appropriate.			
2. Is aware of his/her reactions in a clinical setting.			

Comments: ....
....

B. INTERPERSONAL SKILLS

	UNSAT.	SATIS.	EXCELLENT
1. Is comfortable with patients/clients in clinical setting.			
2. Interacts comfortably with O.T. staff			
3. Is comfortable working with persons of varied ages and social and ethnic groups.			

Comments: ....
....

C. PARTICIPATION IN SUPERVISORY PROCESS

	UNSAT.	SATIS.	EXCELLENT
1. Is able to articulate learning needs.			
2. Asks appropriate questions.			

Comments: ....
....

D. OBSERVATION SKILLS

	UNSAT.	SATIS.	EXCELLENT
1. Describes patient/client behavior objectively following observations.			

Comments: ....
....

E. COMMUNICATION SKILLS

	UNSAT.	SATIS.	EXCELLENT
1. Speaks in clear, concise and well-organized manner.			

Comments: ....
....

F.	UNDERSTANDING THEORETICAL KNOWLEDGE			
1.	Can identify the role of the O.T.R. within the O.T. Department in a health care setting.			
2.	Identifies the significance of activities used in the O.T. treatment process.			
3.	Demonstrates a beginning level of understanding of medical terminology used within the clinical population served.			

Comments: ....
....

G.	PROFESSIONAL BEHAVIOR			
1.	Arrives on days and hours scheduled.			
2.	Notifies supervisor prior to absence or lateness.			
3.	Dresses appropriately and is well groomed.			
4.	Recognizes and follows formal and informal procedures of the department.			
5.	Follows instructions.			
6.	Completes assigned tasks.			
7.	Recognizes patient's/client's right to confidentiality.			
8.	Takes initiative in seeking out new learning experiences.			
9.	Overall, demonstrates appropriate in the clinical setting.			
10.	Demonstrates an appropriate level of interest in working with patients/clients.			

Comments: ....
....

Please comment on this student's potential within the profession of occupational therapy.

Supervisor's Signature _____ Date _____

Student's Signature _____ Date _____

APPENDIX B

FIELDWORK LEVEL I SUPERVISOR'S FINAL ASSESSMENT
OF STUDENT'S PERFORMANCE

_____   O.T. 4920 Seminar I: Psychosocial Dysfunction

_____   O.T. 4921 Seminar II: Physical Dysfunction

_____   O.T. 4922 Seminar III: Developmental Dysfunction

Student _____ Supervisor _____

Clerkship Facility _____

Number of Absences _____ Reason _____ Days Made Up _____

INSTRUCTIONS FOR SUPERVISOR: This evaluation provides important
feedback for the student and the instructor. Your rating will be
converted to a letter grade and will count 10% of the student's
final grade in the Seminar.

Please rate this student within the context of a Fieldwork Level I
experience.

Please check each item using the following rating scale.

(R) Rarely   Given 10 opportunities, the student displayed
                     this behavior less than 2 times.

(O) Occasionally   Given 10 opportunities, the student displayed
                     this behavior 2 or 3 times.

(H) Half the time   Given 10 opportunities, the student displayed
                     this behavior 4, 5, or 6 times.

(F) Frequently   Given 10 opportunities, the student displayed
                     this behavior 7 or 8 times.

(C) Consistently   Given 10 opportunities, the student displayed
                     this behavior 9 or 10 times.

(N) Not applicable

THE STUDENT DEMONSTRATES:	R	O	H	F	C	N
A. SELF AWARENESS						
Is able to recognize & discuss his/her own feelings, attitudes & behavior						
Is aware of his/her reactions in a clinical setting						
Comments:						
B. INTERPERSONAL SKILLS						
Is comfortable with patients/ clients in clinical setting						
Interacts comfortably with O.T. staff						
Is comfortable working with persons of varied ages and social and ethnic groups						
Is able to "hear" and deal appropriately with feedback from patients/clients						
Recognizes maladaptive behavior of patients/clients						
Makes appropriate response to maladaptive behavior						
Comments:						

C. PARTICIPATION IN THE SUPERVISORY PROCESS						
Is able to articulate learning needs & issues of concern						
Is able to utilize feedback from supervisor and staff						
Is able to give feedback to supervisor and staff						
Show a positive attitude toward and is actively engaged in problem-solving						
Is actively involved in the supervisory process						
Asks appropriate questions						

Comments: ....
....

D. OBSERVATION AND INTERVIEWING SKILLS						
Describes patient/client behavior accurately, objectively and in appropriate detail						
Uses interviewing skills to elicit necessary information						

Comments: ....
....

E. COMMUNICATION SKILLS						
Speaks and verbally reports in clear, concise & well-organized manner						
Writes notes, reports & other assignments in clear, concise & well-organized manner						

Comments: ....
....

F. APPLICATION OF THEORETICAL KNOWLEDGE						
Demonstrates understanding of patient's/client's clinical condition & its impact upon occupational performance						
Is developing skill in the selection & use of evaluative tools, & in the recording of evaluative data						
Is developing skill in selecting, utilizing & adapting therapeutic activities to achieve the goals of the patient's/client's treatment program						
Is developing group leadership skills						

Comments: ....
....

G. PERSONAL/PROFESSIONAL BEHAVIOR						
Arrives on days & hours scheduled						
Notifies supervisor prior to absence or lateness						
Dresses appropriately and is well groomed						
Recognizes and follows formal & informal procedures of the department						
Prepares work routine for self scheduling appropriate time for preparation & completion of tasks						
Appears to have done adequate personal preparation for clinical assignments (i.e. is familiar with chart, assessment tool, etc.)						

Recognizes patient's/client's right to confidentiality						
Takes initiative in seeking out new learning experiences						
Overall demonstrates appropriate attitude in the clinical setting						
Demonstrates an appropriate level of interest in dealing with patients						

Comments: ....
....

Please list student's areas of strength.

Please list suggested areas for continued learning.

In your opinion, is the student ready for Fieldwork Level II in this area?   _____

If your answer is "no" or "maybe", please indicate your reasons below.

Supervisor's signature _____ Date _____

Student's signature _____ Date _____

Summary

Michael Knight and Denise Gallaro

It seems appropriate in this summary to restate the reasons for developing a portfolio assessment process.

The purpose of portfolio assessment is to enable faculty to assess the progress of individual students and the effects of programs across the broad spectrum of student development. That is, for students experiencing college, what portfolio information might we/should we gather in order to provide them with feedback that will improve their performance and positively influence their attitudes and perspectives toward themselves, toward others, and expand their career opportunities and life.

In a somewhat similar manner, faculties need to gather information, over time, related to the significant goals and objectives of their educational programs. Just as portfolio information is gathered about individuals to provide a basis for determining student growth and development, an assessment approach that gathers a variety of student work samples in a sequential manner can be used as a diagnostic tool to examine the educational program and make recommendations to enhance the quality of that program.

According to Forrest (1990), a major purpose of engaging in program evaluation is to improve the program. A logical first steps for any institution might be to begin to determine or define the program. Three common conceptions can be identified:

1.   Coursework only -- institutions would seek information on only these courses and would use that information in structuring course requirements, designing courses, and modifying teaching styles.

2.   Courses plus selected out-of-class activities -- evaluate the influence of out-of-class experiences on the achievement of other academic goals.

3.   *All* elements of the college experience -- general education, elective coursework, coursework in the major field, extra-curricular activities are essential to achievement.

As this effort has evolved, there have been numerous modifications in our approach. These modifications are categorized in the four sections that follow this introduction.

>Portfolio Assessment - A Broad Definition
>The Uses of Portfolio Assessment
>Portfolio Assessment and Program Improvement
>Observations and Conclusions

Portfolio Assessment - A Broad Definition

Examination of the chapters in this book reveals an extensive variety of student work samples, performances, documents and activities that fit the particular needs of the program to assess its' effectiveness. In addition, the many methods, procedures and schedules of collecting, storing and analyzing the information demonstrate the varying needs of each program. A further expansion of portfolio analysis is the systematic use of student self-assessment along with the participation of practicing professionals as a means to insure appropriate objectives and standards. These two groups have also contributed to the integration of the curriculum and the integration by students of their learning experiences.

A number of practical considerations influences the development of each programs' assessment process. While the first consideration was always the effectiveness of the effort as evidenced by program improvement and improved student performance, the problems of efficiency arose very quickly. The consistent response of the faculty to this problem was the identification of the higher goals of the program and the creation of complex tasks that provided the opportunity for students to demonstrate and faculty to assess several objectives using a single performance.

The decisions regarding the number of "pieces" included in the portfolio, responsibility for collection and storage, and the setting of standards were made by the faculty in each program with the necessary training and support. These decisions reflected the programs' purpose for assessment and further broadened the definition of portfolio assessment.

The Uses of Portfolios

While there were several applications of portfolio assessment that seemed obvious at the beginning of our effort (uses in accreditation and program review, program analysis and improvement, diagnosis of the growth or problems of individual students, demonstration to students of their own growth, enhanced employment opportunities) a number of additional uses and results were identified.

1. Faculty developed a deeper understanding of their programs' structure and how this structure could be communicated to students enabling the students to see the relationships among courses and understand the sequential development of their knowledge and skills.

2. The decisions associated with portfolio development generally moved the curriculum toward the highest and most complex goals.

3. Several programs combined the use of assessment as a process for student and program improvement with its use as an instructional tool in their curriculum. A highly positive and productive combination of process and product.

4. The availability of portfolios provided an advisement tool used in the selection of electives and the sequencing of coursework students used their sessions to add to the purposes of advisement. Questions went beyond "What courses do I take next?"

   Typical questions included:

   "What student organizations should I join?"
   "What professional organizations should I join?"
   "How can I begin networking?"
   "How can I add to my portfolio?"

Students used this opportunity to address concerns that they have had for many years but were uncertain of the appropriate source of information.

Portfolio Assessment and Program Improvement

Some of the primary benefits, as reported by faculty of portfolio development and analysis can be grouped in the following ways; classroom practices, student satisfaction, and curriculum.

Classroom Practices

- The ability to more clearly communicate my expectations

- An understanding of the importance of key concepts and vocabulary

- Improvement in my ability to assess students' improvement

- An understanding of the relationship between assessment and student performance

- The understanding of how my course contributes to the goals of the program

Student Satisfaction

- The improved communication of program goals and expectations, and career and graduate school opportunities

- A view that faculty are more accessible to students

- Improvements in program handbooks and other printed materials

- Significant modifications in the advisement process

Curriculum

- Improved communication regarding program goals and expectations

- Creation of recommended course-taking patterns

- Implementation of numerous senior seminars to provide an integrating experience
- An increased emphasis on both written and oral communications

- A clear understanding of the relationships among expectations, performance, and evaluation

- The clear focus on learning and the resulting emphasis on student performance

Observations and Conclusions

There has been an emphasis on reflection by students examining their present efforts/products and their longer term goals for development. Some programs require relatively uniform portfolios while others encourage a high degree of diversity. The relationship of the students' performance to the goals of the program is always the consistent measure.

The identification of specific weaknesses allowed for the design of specific plans to target the weakness, whether the performance of an individual student or a particular program was being examined.

Operational definitions of Portfolio Assessment by the faculty who are closest to the effort and best understand the goals of their program and the purpose of assessment have produced the process which is rigorous and generates useful information.